Praise for
CREATE YOUR BEST LEGACY:

"Creating the right estate plan is the most important and basic part of any financial plan. Sometimes it feels that most attorneys make things so complicated that people don't know where to start. In her book, Michelle simplifies the complex. Following her 4-Step Action Guide, regular people know exactly what they need to do. By sharing stories, Michelle makes estate planning easy and digestible. For anyone who has assets and people they care about, this book is a 'must read.'"

Rob Black, host of "Rob Black & Your Money" on KRON 4 TV and 1220 AM Radio San Francisco (www.robblack.com)

"Estate planning laws have changed drastically and new strategies must be discussed and implemented. Too many people have documents that are out of date, confusing and lack protection for their children from divorce and lawsuits. This book is an easy to understand source for long-term strategies that can protect the assets that you have worked so hard to accumulate."

Chad Burton, Certified Financial Planner™ Chief Executive Officer, NewFocus Financial Group (newfocusfinancial.com)

"California is a state with complex and sometimes unusual property and inheritance laws. Combine California's laws with the federal gift and estate tax regime, and it creates an almost indecipherable mess for those California residents attempting to plan for the distribution of their assets at death. Michelle Lerman's new book does a wonderful job of untangling the interplay between California and federal law, while giving understandable and common sense explanations for why things should ideally be ordered in certain ways for California residents. Her book will also be a great tool for those considering a move to the Golden State. The folks who read Michelle Lerman's new book will be several important steps ahead by the time they sit down with their estate planners to discuss the disposition of their most valuable assets."

Jay D. Adkisson, Forbes.com's *Wealth Preservation* columnist

"As the founder of Noah's Bagels and Bread & Circus and as a business consultant, I understand the importance not only of having sound wealth management strategies, but also taking action and implementing those strategies. Estate planning is an indispensable part of any wealth management plan and Michelle's book is a must read for everybody, from novice to seasoned professional, who wants to learn more about this important topic."

Noah Alper, founder of Noah's Bagels and Bread & Circus, author of *Business Mensch: Timeless Wisdom for Today's Entrepreneur*, business consultant (www.noahalperconsulting.com)

"Michelle does an excellent job of taking a complex topic and making it understandable by using plain English, case studies, "take away" summaries, checklists, forms, diagrams, flowcharts. This is a great reference book for anybody interested in this topic, whether you're a layperson or a wealth planning professional."

William Bronchick, best-selling author, attorney, and host of www.legalwiz. com

"*Create Your Best Legacy* does a wonderful job of showing us that we all will leave some kind of legacy. Some will leave a legacy of acrimony and spouses and children wondering why you didn't plan better. Others will leave a legacy of wealth, and thoughtful planning that could impact generations to come, a legacy where your grandchildren's grandchildren find themselves thanking you for your kindness and generosity. This book can change lives."

Adiel Gorel, President of International Capital Group (www.icgre.com), real estate investor, author of *Remote Controlled Real Estate Riches: The Busy Person's Guide To Real Estate Investing*, speaker

"This book should be required reading for individuals concerned about managing their wealth for themselves and their family. Michelle's "4-Step Action Guide" will be invaluable for me and the other members of my family. I believe there are important lessons you will learn from this book that could help you avoid costly mistakes. I give this book my highest recommendation. Thanks for writing this!"

Gene Trowbridge, attorney (www.syndicationlawyers.com), CCIM, author of *It's a Whole New Business*, speaker, teacher

"Michelle Lerman's book, *Create Your Best Legacy,* is a comprehensive compendium of the important issues surrounding estate planning, especially in California. Michelle has illuminated and simplified the sometimes arcane and complex subject of estate planning. I would highly recommend Create Your Best Legacy to anyone involved in or interested in this important element of retirement planning and wealth management."

Tom Anderson, PENSCO Trust Company Founder & Vice Chairman, President of Retirement Industry Trust Association

"Ms. Lerman translates estate planning into plain English and inspires the reader to create an estate plan NOW, rather than leaving one's legacy to an unknown end. By breaking down estate planning into four manageable tasks, *Create Your Best Legacy* empowers the reader to face what would otherwise be a daunting task. This book is a practical guide for both the layman and the lawyer. The chapters are concise and provide clear definitions, illuminating anecdotes and insightful reminders to reconsider outdated estate planning tools in light of recent changes in the law."

Romy S. Taubman, attorney, Partner at Greene, Jordan & Taubman LLP (www.marinfamilylawattorneys.com), specializing in family law, divorce, child custody, child support

"Create Your Best Legacy is filled with insightful words of wisdom, practical advice and easy solutions to avoid disputes before they begin. As a mediator of, among other things, probate disputes, I see firsthand how important it is for families to engage in the thoughtful and transparent estate planning Michelle discusses in her 4-Step Guide. Michelle truly is an "attorney with heart."

Stephen H. Sulmeyer, J.D., Ph.D., attorney, mediator (www.stevesulmeyer.com)

CREATE YOUR BEST LEGACY:

What Every Homeowner,
Real Estate Investor
and Parent Must Know
About Estate Planning,
Living Trusts and Probate

CREATE YOUR BEST LEGACY:

What Every Homeowner, Real Estate Investor and Parent Must Know About Estate Planning, Living Trusts and Probate

4-STEP ACTION GUIDE

INCLUDING EFFECTIVE STRATEGIES

FOR NEW PORTABILITY LAWS

By Michelle C. Lerman,
Attorney at Law
Certified Specialist in Estate Planning, Trust and Probate Law
by the California State Bar Board of Legal Specialization

Published by:

INVESTOR EDUCATION INSTITUTE SERIES, a separate series of Jemic Enterprises, LLC, A Delaware series limited liability company
All rights reserved.

ISBN: 0692253300
ISBN 13: 9780692253304
Investor Education Institute Series, a separate series of Jemic Enterprises, LLC, A Delaware series limited liability company

This book is intended to assist readers as a learning aid but does not constitute tax or legal advice. It is not written (nor is it intended to be used) for purposes of avoiding penalties under the Internal Revenue Code, nor to promote, market, or recommend any transaction or matter addressed. Diligent effort was made to ensure the accuracy of the information in this book, but the author assumes no responsibility for any reader's reliance on any planning discussed in this book and encourages all readers to verify all items by reviewing all original sources before applying them. Further, the factual scenarios have been changed to protect the identity and privacy of clients. Estate planning is fact driven and must be tailored to each situation. The reader should consider all tax and other consequences of any planning technique discussed and seek the advice of an attorney before embarking on any planning discussed in this book.

ACKNOWLEDGMENTS

Thank you to my husband, Jeff, who is my inspiration in business and in life. This book would never have come to fruition without him. He directed the process every step of the way. Jeff—you have empowered me with your support and love these past 32 years. To my mom and dad—thank you for always believing in me. No one could possibly have more remarkable and influential role models! To my mother-in-law, Miriam Lerman, who passed away right before this book was published, thank you for your love and for always believing in me. My deep gratitude to Joseph Fogel for his insightful, creative ideas and indispensable skill in editing this book. Joe—you are brilliant. I could never have finished this book without you. Thank you! And thank you to my Aunt, Pam Bennish, and to the devoted paralegals at our law firm, Cynthia Barbaccia, Katy Strattan, and Erin Morales, for their thoughtful and valuable input. With your help and the support of all our devoted staff, I've been able to memorialize decades of experience in this book so that others can benefit. Thank you from the bottom of my heart.

TABLE OF CONTENTS

STEP #1:   DETERMINE WHETHER YOU NEED AN ESTATE PLAN

STEP #2:   SET YOUR ESTATE PLANNING GOALS

STEP #3:   ESTATE PLANNING BOOT CAMP: WHAT EVERYBODY MUST KNOW

STEP #4: GET IT DONE! DECIDE WHETHER TO DO IT YOURSELF OR HIRE AN ATTORNEY

PREFACE

I always wanted to be a lawyer. My mom and dad, who went to work at a very young age and never graduated from high school, stressed the importance of education and inspired me to follow my dreams. They taught me more than any textbook can about creating a meaningful life and legacy.

My parents came from poor immigrant families. When my mom was 16 and my dad was 21, they married. My dad started off selling flowers on the corner, and then opened a flower shop. Soon after, my dad and one of his customers started building apartments, while my mom handled the day-to-day work at the flower shop. From one flower shop to three, and from a 4-unit to an 8-unit, and to 200-unit apartment complexes, my parents achieved the American Dream. Now married over 60 years, my dad still works in his real estate business, while my mom devotes endless hours to charitable organizations striving to make the world a better place.

My parents raised my sister, brother and me to be financially responsible, hard-working, charitable and passionate about what we do. Through their example, my parents empowered us to develop our *own* legacy, and ensured that their work ethic would affect the world far beyond their years on this earth.

Planning a legacy should be an inclusive, collaborative affair that brings families closer. Consider talking to your family about your estate planning goals, sharing your work life with them, and articulating what you want for their future. By creating an estate plan that embodies your deepest values, you will leave a meaningful and lasting legacy for generations to come.

The wrong estate plan can impact families permanently. It can waste inherited money and destroy relationships. I've seen sisters fighting over whether to sell the family home—a feud that ruined their bond forever. I've seen siblings fighting over their father's care, spending tens of thousands of dollars in court. I've seen siblings going to court over the Christmas decorations that had adorned their childhood home.

By using the 4-Step approach in this book, I have helped hundreds of clients create estate plans that minimize expenses at death, distribute assets according to the clients' wishes and prevent family feuds. I hope this book helps you *CREATE YOUR BEST LEGACY.*

INTRODUCTION

Many people lack the essential legal documents to avoid disputes after they die. In California alone, 42,781 cases were filed in probate court for the fiscal year 2011-2012, according to the 2013 Court Statistics Report published by the Judicial Council of California. With a proper estate plan, most of those cases might never have been filed.

While you might at first think that a book on estate planning is too complicated, you'll learn that reading this guide is much less complicated than dying or becoming disabled without an estate plan for safeguarding assets and protecting family. One of my friends died at 50 after suffering from a massive heart attack. He died without life insurance or an estate plan, leaving his wife and teenage children with the complicated task of fending for themselves.

Sooner or later, documents are needed. Creating them ahead of time is generally much less complicated and costly. A court proceeding after death or incapacity is much more complicated and expensive than creating an estate plan proactively.

You might think you are too busy to read a book about estate planning. Perhaps you don't want to spend the money to create an estate plan. Bill died at his company's holiday party when he was 58. Like so many, he died without an estate plan. His financial planner said he'd given Bill my contact information years ago. Perhaps Bill had been too busy because he never called me. Because Bill had not created an estate plan, the law created one for him. Bill's house, where his sister and her children lived, went to his estranged father, leaving Bill's sister and her children homeless. Instead of spending $2,500 for a Living Trust, Bill's estate paid over $50,000 in legal fees, court costs, and expenses during the one and a half years it took to settle the estate in court. Spending money on an estate plan now will save money later.

Sometimes people don't create an estate plan because they don't have anyone to name as the guardian to care for their kids or someone to handle their money if they become incapacitated. But that's a misguided excuse because, if you don't choose, a judge will decide for you. Even if you are not completely comfortable

with your options, any decision you make will probably be better than leaving your children's destiny to a stranger.

Not having time to start an estate plan is like not having time to replace a leaky roof. Both are critical to safeguarding your assets and protecting your family, and if you don't take responsibility you'll end up with a huge mess. If you don't set your affairs in order before you die, someone else will be stuck spending the time and money to handle the assets. By planning your estate before you die, you will protect your family after you die.

Many people are confused and misinformed. They don't know what they need to know. Often what they do know is wrong. This straightforward, 4-Step Action Guide explains how to create an estate plan that protects your assets during your lifetime and after your death, and reduces unnecessary taxes, attorney's fees and court fees. The "life lessons" and true stories—including some nightmares (with names and circumstances changed for privacy)—presented on these pages offer cautionary tales to help you avoid making the same mistakes.

Where other estate planning books read like an encyclopedia, this guide focuses on key points, and answers the most critical questions simply, without extensive legalese. The "Take-Away" sections at the end of each chapter summarize what you need to know.

Importantly, this book explains the impact of the American Taxpayer Relief Act, which went into effect in January 2013, and how and why estate plans must change in light of the new "permanent" law. For years we often created a Living Trust that included a "Bypass Trust." After passage of the Taxpayer Relief Act, an "All to Spouse Plan with Optional Disclaimer Trust" or "QTIP-Protection Trust" should now be the center-piece of estate plans for many couples. Those with existing estate plans will learn what to review, and every reader will learn how the new law affects estate planning, the potential disasters inherent in the Bypass Trust, and how to avoid them.

This 4-Step Action Guide will help you safeguard your assets and protect your family. I have used this 4-Step approach for years and it works. If you are confused, if you think estate planning is a daunting task, and if you have no idea where to begin, start by reading this guide. For those who know that estate planning is more than just a tax plan for the wealthy, reading this 4-Step Action Guide will teach you about love, life and legacy, and help get your affairs in order—before it's too late.

ATTENTION: CRITICAL INFORMATION FOR CALIFORNIA RESIDENTS OR OWNERS OF CALIFORNIA REAL PROPERTY:

While most of the information in this 4-Step Action Guide pertains to all U.S. citizens or residents, this book also includes critical information for California residents and owners of real property in California. You will learn how to avoid losing your property under California's community property laws, how to pass on low property taxes to your family, how to avoid court delays caused by reduced court operating hours and California's budget problems, and how to avoid California's statutory probate fees, which are based on the gross value of the estate, which can be relatively high value if the estate includes California real property.

One California man lost half of his assets because he didn't understand California's community property laws. One man passed on real property that his partner couldn't afford because his property taxes skyrocketed. One woman's assets were tied up in California court for months and large chunks of the inheritance went to the lawyers instead of to her family. You'll read these stories and more in this guide, and learn how to avoid these disastrous consequences that could impact you and your family for years and generations to come.

HOW TO USE THIS GUIDE

This guide is divided into four main sections, or steps, each answering a critical question in the estate planning process:

Step #1: Do I need an estate plan?

Step #2: What can my estate plan do for me?

Step #3: What do I need to know to get the right estate plan?

Step #4: How do I get my plan done?

To get a full picture of the process, read each step from start to finish. If one of the questions above is of particular interest, then find that step number in the table of contents and read that section to get your questions answered. For a short answer to each question, turn directly to the end of the section and review the **"TAKE AWAY,"** an easy-to-read summary of the most critical information for each step in the estate planning process.

If you learn best through stories, then peruse the **vignettes** within each step to learn from the experience of others. Each vignette is labeled and shown in italics in the Table of Contents. The **"Life Lessons,"** highlighted in grey throughout the guide, give further flavor to the teachings within a section—words of wisdom you might not find in a typical estate planning book.

For an overview and simple explanation of key words, refer to the **"Glossary"** at the end of the book. You won't find legalese. You will find clear explanations of estate planning terms that you will want to know, making it easier to read the guide.

For visual learners, the book offers **diagrams** of the three types of Living Trusts discussed in this guide, a chart discussing the pros and cons of specific lifetime gifting opportunities, a sample death beneficiary designation and an estate plan review checklist.

California residents will also find valuable and free resources in the relevant portions of the book.

Whether you decide to read this 4-Step Guide from page 1 to the end, or to look at the table of contents to determine which topics will be most helpful, you will find what you need to CREATE YOUR BEST LEGACY.

DETERMINE WHETHER YOU NEED AN ESTATE PLAN

Don't Die Dumb: Get SMART

You might think that a book on estate planning is too complicated. It's nothing compared to the complication of dying or becoming disabled without an estate plan for safeguarding assets and protecting family.

After Susan's mother died, she came to my office carrying her two-year-old twins. I could see she had been crying. She was overwhelmed and distraught. On top of being an exhausted mother of twins and mourning the death of her mother, she explained that she was heading into a battle with her stepfather over her mother's house.

When her mother remarried late in life, she thought she had created an estate plan to protect her daughter. Without an attorney, Susan's mother and new husband signed a written agreement that they thought confirmed that all of his property and bank accounts would remain his and that her house, which she owned before marriage, would remain hers. The agreement expressed their intention to leave their assets to their respective children at death. Her mother's husband signed a deed confirming he had no ownership in the house. They took the deed to the county recorder's office to have it recorded as a matter of public record. Susan's

mother signed a document called a Parent-Child Exclusion form attempting to ensure that, when she died, the property taxes on the house would not increase when the house was transferred to Susan. Susan's mother and stepfather even talked openly with their children; when Susan's mother became very ill, she told Susan many times that one day the house would be hers.

Susan's mother thought she had an estate plan that would protect her daughter. She was wrong. Shortly after Susan's mother died, her stepfather hired an attorney, claiming that he was entitled to one-half of the house. He filed an action in court, Susan filed an action in court, and a costly battle ensued.

Sadly, none of the documents Susan's mother signed protected her daughter: not the written agreement, not the deed, and not the exclusion form for property taxes. Those documents stipulated their respective rights during life or in the event of divorce, not what would happen at death. Susan's mother needed an estate plan leaving her assets to her daughter, and she didn't have one.

Had Susan's mother followed this 4-Step Action Guide, she could have easily safeguarded her home and protected her daughter. Instead, she left her daughter in a court battle with her stepfather.

Reading this 4-Step Action Guide enables you to be SMART in creating an estate plan:

> **S**pecific: By setting your goals, you will be clear and *specific* about the <u>outcome</u> you want from your estate plan—i.e., avoid probate court, minimize estate tax, create a binder with all original signed estate planning documents.
> **M**easurable: By completing each step in this guide, you will *measure* your progress in creating an estate plan.
> **A**chievable: Rather than becoming an estate planning expert, you will know the essential information and the right questions to ask so you can *achieve* a plan that safeguards your assets and meets your goals.
> **R**ealistic: Be *realistic* about the plan you want to achieve. Most people should start with a basic estate plan that includes a Living Trust, Will, Durable Power of Attorney and Health Care Directive. Then, consider whether you need additional estate planning (such as an Irrevocable Trust to hold life insurance or your primary residence to

reduce estate tax or add asset protection.) If you tackle too much, you might never create the basic plan that you need.

Timeline: You should be able to read this 4-Step Action Guide and create an estate plan within 2-4 weeks. Commit to your *timeline* below.

TIMELINE

4-STEP ACTION GUIDE	DATE TO BE COMPLETED
STEP #1 Determine need for estate plan	
STEP #2 Establish estate planning goals	
STEP #3 Understand estate planning basic facts	
STEP #4 Get it done!	
RESULT: Estate plan completed and signed	

What Is an Estate Plan and Do You Need One?

GENERAL BENEFITS OF AN ESTATE PLAN

A thoughtful estate plan can accomplish many goals. It minimizes taxes. It enables you to leave a legacy—to make a difference—after you are gone. An estate plan keeps assets in the family in the event of divorce. It explains what you want to happen if you die or become unable to manage your own affairs. If you are in a car accident or contract a terminal illness, your estate plan will authorize someone you choose in advance to protect you and your assets. If you don't create your own plan, the law will create one for you—and it probably won't be the plan you would have wanted.

An estate plan is, in essence, a grouping of legal documents that drastically reduces expense and administrative hassle after death. The plan organizes your life, telling your family what they need to know about your bank accounts, your safe deposit box, your online passwords and your pets' needs. An estate plan organizes all the details of your family's life after your death so that your family can benefit from your love and protection even when you are gone.

PROTECTION FROM CREDITORS

Estate planning is the **most effective** means of protecting your assets against certain creditors, acting like a vaccine against attempts to access the inheritance due to large debts, divorce or business lawsuits. But you must create a Living Trust *before* you die to provide the best protection for your family. Even those with hazard, property and liability insurance should be concerned about protecting assets from creditors because insurance doesn't cover all risks; even when you think you are covered, your insurance company could deny your claim. The courts are full of lawsuits by good people suing their carrier for bad faith denial of their claims made under their policies.

PROTECTING YOUR CHILDREN'S ASSETS

An estate plan can protect assets for children by preventing a surviving spouse from leaving all the assets to a new spouse instead of to the kids. A properly drafted estate plan that transfers assets at death to a non-changeable, lifetime trust for children can also (1) prevent the assets from going to your children's divorcing spouse, or (2) protect the assets so that your children can't squander their inheritance.

PROTECTION FOR BUSINESS OWNERS

An estate plan can address the unique concerns of business owners:

- ❖ Who will manage the business if you are disabled?
- ❖ Who will run the business after you die?
- ❖ How will the cash needs of the business be met?
- ❖ How do you divide the estate fairly between all children when only one child runs the business and the business is the primary asset in the estate?

Insurance often plays an important role in estate planning for business owners. Without insurance, the business might not have the cash needed to pay for ongoing management of the business or to buy out family members who won't be involved in the running of the business. By putting the title of the business into a Living Trust, business owners can appoint the right person to handle everything without court intervention. With proper estate planning, a business can stay within the family for generations or can be sold to support the surviving loved ones.

Business owners should also consider a written agreement with the other partners for a buy-out upon the death of one partner. Otherwise, business owners might be in business with their partner's family, who might not be compatible with you and might not let you sell your share if your family needs cash for living expenses.

Business owners almost always need an estate plan to avoid court involvement and to detail the business succession plan that will stipulate who will run and own the business.

LIFE LESSONS:

- ❖ **Passwords:** *No matter what you ultimately decide about your estate planning, create a good system for storing your passwords – now! Whether it's your online banking password or the password for your frequent flyer miles, keep passwords secure and accessible to someone else in case something happens to you. Download MasterLockVault.com or another suitable program to keep your passwords in a safe place. If you are married, establish one joint account for both you and your spouse so that you both know each other's passwords.*
- ❖ **Pets:** *Talk to your friends and family about your pets and determine who would care for them if something happens to you. In addition, create a plan for paying for the expenses of caring for your pets. In California, consider a pet trust.*

> ❖ **Safe Deposit Box:** *If you keep anything in a safe deposit box, and especially if you keep your estate plan there, give someone access. And be sure that person knows where the safe-deposit box is located!*

What Happens if You Don't Have an Estate Plan?

A CAUTIONARY TALE; BAD THINGS HAPPEN TO GOOD PEOPLE

In my law practice, I'm reminded daily how bad things happen to good people who don't have an estate plan. One couple owned their home as "Joint Tenants," meaning that when one spouse dies, the house passes to the survivor without probate court. The wife died, and the house passed by law to her husband. After her husband died, the son called me for help with transferring the title of the house to him. The son's nightmare started when he realized that, because his dad had two older daughters from a prior marriage, the son wasn't getting the house. The house would have to be sold and the proceeds split between him and his two half-sisters. Instead of inheriting the house that he grew up in and in fact still lived in when his dad died, the son will only get 1/3 of the proceeds from the sale of the house, and he will be left searching for somewhere to live.

Without an estate plan in place, you, your assets, and your family are vulnerable and unprotected. Grief, confusion, frustration, stress, and a mountain of administrative chores collide after a death, often leading to family feuds and legal complications. Without proper estate planning, the consequences can be severe. Your assets could be unnecessarily squandered in court and attorney fees. Relationships can be destroyed while your family fights over the distribution of your assets or the custody of your children.

WASTED MONEY: FEES FOR CONSERVATORS, ATTORNEYS AND PROBATE

If you don't have an estate plan and you have significant assets (in California that currently means your assets are worth more than $150,000 not including jointly held bank accounts, real estate titled as "Joint Tenants" or an IRA/401k with a beneficiary designation), a judge typically decides who receives the assets in a procedure known as "Probate," usually costing tens of thousands of dollars more than creating an estate plan. Without an estate plan, you are likely to experience higher expenses, more delay and a loss of control over your assets, and you'll be stuck with the default estate plan provided under the law.

Without an estate plan a judge may appoint a "Conservator" to take control of your assets that you are not able to manage if you become incapacitated. Your assets will then be used to pay court costs, attorney's fees, Conservator's fees, and fees for the attorney representing the Conservator. That's a lot of attorneys and a lot of fees that could have been avoided by establishing an estate plan.

> *Sibling Rivalry Goes to Court:* A brother and sister went to court over their mother's personal care and finances. The court battle was a matter of public record, there for the whole world to see. The court appointed a Conservator whom the mother had never met. The Conservator petitioned the court for over $30,000 in fees. The attorney for the Conservator asked the court for over $25,000 in fees. The brother asked for over $11,000 in fees, and the sister asked for over $20,000 to pay her attorney and over $1,000 to pay for her costs. They all fought over the right to collect the fees. The court used the mother's assets to pay these bills.

An estate plan can also settle family feuds before they begin, saving exorbitant legal fees. While any court battle is expensive, court battles over an inheritance produce the added expense of emotional distress. By identifying the possible "troublemakers," the right estate plan reduces the chances that heirs will interfere with your goals.

Someone once told me that he didn't have enough assets to worry about creating an estate plan. The truth is, the people who do not have a lot of assets are often the ones who can't afford <u>not</u> to have an estate plan. All individuals with assets should consider an estate plan. It's almost always less expensive and less complicated to die with an estate plan than without one. Failing to create a plan or update an existing plan wastes money and distributes your assets in unintended ways.

> *The Procrastinator Paid the Price:* Before Diane died, she met with an estate planning attorney to update her estate plan. However, she never signed the new documents. She reviewed various drafts, each

with slightly different names and percentages, but not one person in those drafts received a single thing. Because no one named in Diane's old estate plan survived her, and she didn't have a Living Trust, the law created a plan for her—a terrible plan.

It was expensive: $80,000 of Diane's money went to the attorneys, the court-appointed "administrator" and the court-appointed "probate referee" who appraised Diane's assets. Perhaps even worse, Diane didn't know the people receiving the rest of her assets: The court ordered one-half of the assets to go to her estranged stepdaughter (who died before receiving her share, so that "inheritance" went to the administrator of her probate estate) and the other half to go to a relative that Diane had never met—a half-blood niece in a foreign country who was the daughter of Diane's deceased half-sister. Because Diane's stepdaughter died without any estate plan before receiving her share, we opened another court proceeding to probate the stepdaughter's assets. Months later, one-half of Diane's assets were transferred to her stepgrandchildren, whom Diane had never even met.

Diane could have saved $70,000 if she had put her assets into a Living Trust. Instead of spending $5,000 to create a Living Trust and $5,000 to administer her Living Trust without involving the court, she (or rather her estate) spent over $80,000 going to court. Not one dollar went to one person named in her draft estate plan. Her money went to strangers.

LOSS OF CONTROL OVER HEALTH CARE

If you are unable to manage your money and assets yourself, then estate plans designate a person of your choice to handle your money and assets according to your wishes and in support of your health and other needs. Estate plans ensure that you enter the end-of-life stage with the health care you want and with the dignity you deserve. Everyone needs an estate plan, even if it only consists of instructions about health care in the case of a coma or terminal illness. Had 41-year-old Terri Schiavo created an estate plan before she collapsed in her home and went into a coma, her family might not have spent seven years fighting in court about whether to remove her feeding tube. Terri should have signed a Health Care Directive putting someone in charge of making her decisions and confirming whether she wanted to be connected to a feeding tube.

LOSS OF PRIVACY

If you pass away or become incapacitated without an estate plan, the court will intervene and all court proceedings and records become available to the public. An estate plan can make sure your affairs remain private.

> *Soprano Exposed.* Within hours after actor James Gandolfini died, his estate documents were filed in a New York court as required by law. Soon after, his Will was posted on the internet for prying eyes. It is doubtful the 51-one-year-old actor of the acclaimed HBO series *The Sopranos* intended for his private estate plan to be scrutinized by anybody with internet access.

What are the Benefits of a Living Trust?

People who own assets—like a home and bank accounts, especially California residents or those with real property in California—should consider creating a document called a Living Trust to avoid the time and expense of having the court manage your affairs. Assets that are titled so that they are owned by someone called a "Trustee" can pass at death without court intervention. You, not the court, stay in control.

You choose the person in charge, *you* choose what the person can and cannot do and *you* choose who inherits your assets and how. In other words, when you create an estate plan with a Living Trust, the person or institution *you choose* distributes your assets to those *you name* in your Living Trust when you die. Without the Living Trust, most assets—except those with named beneficiaries such as life insurance, retirement accounts, and property held as joint tenancy—require a judge to oversee the management and distribution of the assets upon incapacity or death.

An estate plan with a Living Trust is usually simple to create and won't affect your property taxes or the way you report income on your income tax return. You pay no annual fee to maintain a Living Trust, and you can easily move assets in and out of a Living Trust, usually without an attorney. Plus, a Living Trust is flexible because you can change it until your death or incapacity.

An estate plan that includes a Living Trust generally keeps your affairs out of the courts if you die or become incapacitated. On the other hand, without proper estate planning, the court will intervene and the court proceedings and records will enter the public domain. In addition to keeping matters private and saving time and

money, a Living Trust allows the Trustee *you appoint* to manage your assets if you become incapacitated. The bottom line: For anyone owning a home in California, establishing a Living Trust is the biggest no-brainer in wealth management.

Is "Will Power" Enough? The Pitfalls of an Estate Plan with ONLY a Will and No Living Trust

Some estate plans only include a Will, and other estate plans include both a Will and a Living Trust. The main difference between the two plans is the likelihood of court intervention.

While both a Will and a Living Trust explain who gets what, funding assets into a Living Trust avoids the time and expense of probate court; with a Living Trust, the Trustee has the power to transfer the assets without the need for the court to control the transfer. On the other hand, having only a Will makes it much more likely that a judge will supervise the distribution of the assets (unless all the assets are held either jointly as "Joint Tenants" or held with named beneficiaries, in which case assets can be transferred after death by an automatic right of survivorship rather than court involvement).

People with assets generally need more than a Will; they need a Living Trust to reduce the chance of court intervention during their lifetime and after their death.

The Pitfalls of Living Trusts (What Most Lawyers Won't Tell You)

Despite the benefits of a Living Trust, creating an estate plan with a Living Trust in addition to a Will has four main pitfalls:

1. **Complexity**. An estate plan with a Living Trust is more complicated to create than an estate plan consisting of a simple Will because the plan requires the drafting of both the Living Trust and the Will. Because creating a Living Trust does not replace the need for a Will, you will need a Living Trust, which dictates who gets what, and a Will, which nominates a guardian for minor children and instructs that any assets not titled in the Living Trust before death be poured over (hence the name "Pour-Over Will" when used in conjunction with a Living Trust) into the Living Trust after death.

2. **Re-Titling**. Assets generally need to be re-titled into the Living Trust, an added step not required in a Will. Transferring assets into the Living Trust will generally require new account numbers. Automatic deposits and withdrawals will need to be reestablished. Refinancing real property in a Living Trust may necessitate removing and re-titling the real property from the Living Trust, and then again titling the real property back into the Living Trust after the refinancing. See the Appendix for guidance on how to title assets into a living trust for specific asset types.

3. **Expense**. An estate plan with a Living Trust is more expensive to create than an estate plan with only a simple Will. While some states like California provide a Will form along with instructions in their statutes, which can easily be printed and completed, no state that I am aware of provides free Living Trust forms. If using an attorney, you will generally pay more for a Living Trust than for a simple Will.

4. **Lack of Court Supervision**. A Living Trust typically removes the court from the post-death process, but court supervision is preferred in certain circumstances. For example, a terminally ill mother of young children did not want a Living Trust because she wanted the court to supervise the distribution of her small estate. Her simple Will gave her peace of mind, knowing that the court's supervision would protect her family.

LIFE LESSONS:

A Living Trust adds some costs and complexity to an estate plan. The added expense may not be necessary if you are young and your estate consists only of IRAs, 401ks or life insurance policies, which have Beneficiary Designations. Otherwise, especially for those who are older and need proper planning in the event of incapacity, the savings in time and expense of a probate or a conservatorship, and the privacy that a Living Trust affords, almost always outweigh the initial added expense.

What Is an Ethical Will and Do You Need One?

An Ethical Will is a non-legal document, and it's optional. However, here's why you might want one: Your Ethical Will could impact the world for generations to come.

An Ethical Will—which can take the form of a letter, a certificate or even a book— allows you to pour your heart out to your family. You can share what's most

meaningful to you about your life and your hopes and dreams for the next generation. Some Ethical Wills are addressed to children and describe their ancestry or the origin of their names. Some describe dreams for the future, or ways to inspire others. An Ethical Will can ensure that an estate plan is much more than a simple distribution of assets.

> *The Grandfather/The G-dfather:* My friend and client, Nancy, started a high school in San Francisco based on the Ethical Will of her grandfather, who expressed the importance of education. Although Nancy didn't have the financial resources to start the school, she found a smart, caring and philanthropic woman who did, without whom the school never would have gotten off the ground or grown to what it is today. That woman, along with a team of like-minded, dedicated community leaders, created a school that recently celebrated its 13th anniversary of educating students from Marin County, San Francisco, the Peninsula and the East Bay. Graduates have become leaders in the world, impacting the lives of many more.
>
> Through an Ethical Will, Nancy's grandfather impacted the lives of many children who have attended the high school. Think about how your estate plan might inspire your loved ones—it's an empowering thought. Your dreams can become reality long after your time on Earth.

What Estate Planning Do I Need for My IRA, 401k and Life Insurance?

NAMED BENEFICIARIES REQUIRED

People mistakenly believe that if they create a Living Trust or Will, they don't need to do anything else for their retirement accounts and life insurance. However, because a Living Trust and Will generally do not control retirement accounts or life insurance, this misconception can prove costly.

Owners of retirement accounts or life insurance policies must name a beneficiary on the Beneficiary Designation, a document that is not part of a Living Trust or Will. A Beneficiary Designation refers to the document that governs the distribution of life insurance or retirement accounts after death. The Beneficiary Designation, when properly completed, instructs the institution how to distribute the IRA, 401k and life insurance proceeds without court intervention. Individuals with retirement accounts or life insurance, in addition to a Living Trust, also need to name both a primary beneficiary and an alternate beneficiary in case the first-named beneficiary dies.

It's All in the Details: Tony created a Living Trust and Will. However, he did not complete a Beneficiary Designation for his IRA before he died suddenly at the age of 66. Even though he had a Living Trust and a Will, neither avoided the huge fees paid to the attorneys during the nine months in probate court.

Without a Beneficiary Designation, Tony's estate paid for the probate court to administer his retirement account after he died. Even more costly, his heirs paid *income tax* in one lump sum on the full value of the retirement accounts, which would have been avoided had he named his sister on the Beneficiary Designation. **Tony could have avoided the cost of probate court, the nine-month delay, and the huge income tax on the full value of the account**. Tony had a Living Trust, but that wasn't all he needed. He needed to complete a simple, one-page Beneficiary Designation.

LIFE LESSONS—UPDATE YOUR BENEFICIARIES:

People often die with a deceased spouse named on the Beneficiary Designation, or even an ex-spouse or ex-girlfriend! One man I know died with his deceased wife's name on the Beneficiary Designation for his $2 million insurance policy. The insurance was tied up in court for months before the remaining proceeds <u>after</u> payment of all the legal fees were distributed to his estranged kids. Be sure to update your Beneficiary Designations!

LIFE LESSONS—CONSIDER CHARITIES:

Qualified charitable organizations make great beneficiaries of retirement accounts because these charities don't have to pay income tax on the retirement accounts. If you have assets in a Living Trust and an equal value of assets in retirement accounts, rather than leaving the Living Trust 50/50 to individuals and charities, leave the Living Trust assets to the individuals and the retirement accounts to the charities.

LIFE LESSONS—CHOOSE THE RIGHT WORDS:

In estate planning, as in life, we have to choose our words carefully. Seek legal advice when completing a Beneficiary Designation, which will determine who gets the proceeds of an IRA or 401k. Writing the wrong word on the Beneficiary Designation can determine whether the entire account is subject to income tax in the year of death or whether taxes can be stretched out over the life expectancy of the person named. For example, never insert the words "my estate" on a Beneficiary Designation form because the IRS indicates that an "estate" is not a proper designated beneficiary. If "an estate" is named as the beneficiary, the IRS treats the IRA as if no beneficiary were named, with disastrous tax consequences! Filling out a Beneficiary Designation has significant financial and tax consequences so be sure to get legal advice in completing what may look like a simple form. Otherwise, you may be leaving your family a big mess along with the IRA or 401k.

TAX CONSIDERATIONS

Retirement accounts may be subject to both income tax and estate tax at death. Proper planning can reduce both. Owners of retirement accounts can often minimize income tax by naming a spouse as the beneficiary. A spouse will generally be able to defer income tax on an inherited retirement account, whereas a non-spouse pays some income tax in the year after the owner dies. Owners not naming a spouse should consider naming younger beneficiaries who, because they have a longer life expectancy, will be able to stretch out the required payments from the retirement account.

Further, owners of retirement accounts and large estates that might be subject to estate tax must address the potential estate tax on retirement assets in the Living Trust. A Living Trust instructing the estate tax to be paid *from the retirement account* will increase income tax. A Living Trust instructing that the estate tax be paid *from trust assets* could minimize income tax because extra distributions from the retirement account won't be needed to pay the estate tax.

Similarly, with life insurance, a Living Trust must instruct whether the estate tax attributable to life insurance will be paid *from the Living Trust assets* or from everyone's interest in <u>*all*</u> *of the decedent's assets,* both the assets in the Living Trust and the life insurance passing outside it. If the estate tax were paid from the Living Trust, but the insurance is not payable to the Living Trust (simply because the Beneficiary Designation directs it to an individual and not to the Living Trust), one person might receive the life insurance proceeds while another person might have to pay the estate tax on the insurance—an unfair and likely unintended result. Plus, if the life insurance were paid to an individual and not to the Living Trust, there may not be sufficient assets in the trust to pay the tax! A well-drafted estate plan addresses each situation and avoids unintended and unfair results.

SPECIAL CONSIDERATIONS FOR MARRIED COUPLES

Married couples that don't plan carefully for their retirement assets are particularly vulnerable. For example, if Robert had large retirement accounts and named his spouse, Cynthia, on the beneficiary designation form, his kids from his prior marriage might never get the money, even after Cynthia dies: Once Robert dies, Cynthia's chosen beneficiary, who may not be Robert's kids, will get all the remaining retirement accounts.

Spouses typically name each other on the beneficiary designation form for retirement accounts, but those with substantial retirement accounts and children from a prior marriage should seek input from an attorney or tax advisor before naming a spouse on the beneficiary designation. Although married individuals rarely use available estate planning techniques to restrain the discretion of the surviving spouse, those with significant retirement assets or life insurance should educate themselves about the issue. To avoid unintentionally disinheriting their children, owners of retirement accounts can leave the retirement account to their spouse (the stepparent of their children) and leave non-retirement assets directly to their children.

In addition to the Beneficiary Designation that determines the beneficiary, and a thoughtful Living Trust to address tax issues, married individuals with a large estate that includes retirement assets should consider creating a "Spousal Property Agreement"—a written agreement between spouses, separate from the Living Trust, which impacts the division of their assets upon a death. A Spousal Property Agreement could allow more than the deceased spouse's share of the trust assets to remain in a protected trust for the surviving spouse, which could (1) add protection of the trust assets (e.g., from the grasp of a second spouse), and (2) minimize estate tax after the surviving spouse dies.

LIFE LESSONS:

Consult an attorney before signing a Spousal Property Agreement. Otherwise, you might unwittingly relinquish assets that rightfully belong to you.

SPECIAL CONSIDERATIONS FOR CHILDREN

Leaving retirement accounts or life insurance to young children can be tricky. For larger retirement accounts, consider creating a trust for young children for the sole purpose of holding the retirement assets until the children are older. The trust language should be included in or attached to the Beneficiary Designation form.

You can name the Living Trust as the beneficiary (by including the name of the children's subtrust in the Beneficiary Designation Form), but only if the children's trust has been drafted properly to receive retirement assets. Naming the children's trust helps prevent the children from squandering the proceeds.

For maximum income tax efficiency when creating a trust for children with a wide age span, the Beneficiary Designation for retirement accounts should first divide the retirement assets into separate shares, one for each child, and then direct each share to be held in trust. This enables each child to use his or her own life expectancy in calculating how much to be distributed each year, called "Required Minimum Distributions." Because the child will pay income tax on each distribution, the separate share language can minimize income tax, especially when the children are far apart in age.

Proceed cautiously when completing what may seem like a simple fill-in-the-blank beneficiary designation form. Naming the right beneficiary will determine whether the retirement account needs to go through probate court, how much income tax is paid and whether the retirement accounts pass to your kids or your spouse's new spouse. Consult your attorney for more information on naming the children's trust as the beneficiary of a retirement account or life insurance policy, as the details can be complex and confusing and a detailed discussion is beyond the scope of this book. Never name as beneficiary a Living Trust or a children's trust created under the Living Trust without the advice of an attorney.

LIFE LESSONS:

Do not name minor children on any Beneficiary Designation without (1) naming a custodian who will manage the assets for the children under the Uniform Transfers to Minors Act, or (2) creating a trust on the Beneficiary Designation.

In California, you can instruct the custodian to hold the assets until the age of 25. If you don't specify "until age 25," you are out of luck—the children will have full control at 18. I doubt many parents think 18 is a good age for their child to inherit a lot of money!

SAMPLE IRA DEATH BENEFICIARY DESIGNATION NAMING SPOUSE AS PRIMARY BENEFICIARY AND A CUSTODIAN FOR MINOR CHILDREN AS SECONDARY BENEFICIARY

IRA Owner: _____

Social Security Number: _____

Birth Date: _____

Financial Institution (IRA Custodian): _____

Account Number (IRA): _____

Primary Death Beneficiary: Spouse

If IRA Owner's spouse, _____("Spouse"), whose social security number is _____, survives the IRA OWNER, Spouse shall be the beneficiary of 100% of the above-referenced IRA, free of trust.

Alternate Death Beneficiary Designation: Children Outright but to a Custodian if under the age of 25:

If IRA Owner's Spouse fails to survive the IRA OWNER, the above-referenced IRA shall be divided into separate shares of equal market value, one share for each of IRA Owner's surviving children, free of trust; provided, however, if any of IRA Owner's children fail to survive IRA OWNER, but leave issue who survive IRA OWNER, the share of the deceased child shall be divided for said issue in the manner provided in section 240 of the California Probate Code.

Identification of my children:

NAME OF CHILDREN   DATES OF BIRTH

_____   _____

_____   _____

_____   _____

Each share, if any, for a child/issue who has not attained 25 years of age at the IRA OWNER's death shall be held for the benefit of the child/issue by _____, as custodian, under the Uniform Transfers to Minors Act until the child/issue attains 25 years of age, or as long as allowed under the UTMA. If the custodian named above is unable to act, then the share for the child/issue under 25 shall be held by an alternate responsible adult chosen in the sole and absolute discretion of the IRA OWNER's personal representative nominated in the IRA OWNER's Last Will for the sole and absolute benefit of the child/issue under the age of 25.

No Liability for IRA Custodian: The IRA Custodian shall incur no liability to any person interested in the IRA for relying on information provided by or acting upon the written instruction of (i) an agent acting for the IRA OWNER under durable power of attorney, or (ii) a custodian under UTMA/CUTMA acting for an individual entitled to an interest hereunder following the IRA OWNER'S death.

_____   _____
IRA OWNER   DATE

THE TAKE-AWAY FROM STEP #1

An estate plan can save thousands of dollars at death and ensure that you maintain control of your assets. If you don't create an estate plan, the law will impose its own, and it probably will not be the plan you want. Even if your plan consists only of a do-it-yourself Will, it is generally still cheaper, faster, and simpler to create an estate plan than to be stuck with the default legal rules. In Step #1 of this 4-Step Action Guide, you determined whether you need an estate plan. If so (hint: for most anyone with assets or with loved ones, the answer is "Yes"), then it's time to take Step #2: setting your estate planning goals.

STEP #2:

SET YOUR ESTATE PLANNING GOALS

The Importance of Setting Goals

Whether you decide to do it yourself or hire an attorney, your final estate plan will only be as good as the goals you set. You cannot attain successful results until you know what you want to achieve. If you don't know where you're going, odds are you won't reach your destination.

Estate planning is an inspiring process of leaving your legacy in the world. By thinking about the outcome you hope to achieve, you ensure your loved ones will be provided for and your life will continue to impact their lives positively after you are gone. Everyone will leave a legacy. Some do it by intention; others do it by their lack of action. Will yours be a legacy where those you love know you cared enough to plan to make sure they receive as much as possible of your wealth, and where everybody clearly understands your final wishes? Or will you leave a legacy of confusion, disputes, and lawsuits, where your loved ones watch your wealth go unnecessarily to lawyers and courts who will attempt to decipher what you "really wanted" due to your lack of proper planning?

Everyone has different estate planning goals. You may instinctively know yours: "I want to protect my children without spoiling them," for instance. But if you have a second marriage and kids from the first, your goals may not be so clear.

19

Clear Goals + Wise Planning = Solutions: One man had a grown son and a second wife. He didn't have many assets, and he didn't know how to divide them. He felt forced to choose between providing for his son or his wife. He was able to solve his dilemma by purchasing a life insurance policy payable to his wife and leaving all of the trust assets to his son. At first, he struggled to articulate his estate planning goals. Once he realized that his goal was to provide for both his wife and his son, he created a solution.

The "I Love You" Approach: A man diagnosed with cancer and given only two months to live wanted peace of mind knowing that everything would be as simple as possible for his wife. He wanted to make sure that his wife had full control over all assets and the power to make all decisions. He trusted her completely and did not want her to have any restrictions on the assets. We set up an "All to Spouse Plan" (discussed in depth later in the book) with his wife as the only Trustee. When he died, his wife didn't need to hassle with legalities— everything was already titled to her as Trustee of the Living Trust. I called his wife recently to check in. She thanked me again for making the financial part of her husband's passing so seamless; the emotional part, she said, had been so trying that she never could have handled the finances had it not been so simple. This couple needed a flexible and simple estate plan; once that goal was set, they achieved it.

Some people want the simplest estate plan. Others want to minimize estate tax, or control their assets so the surviving spouse doesn't give them away to Don Juan or Sexy Sue, and are willing to accept some complexity to achieve those goals.

Virtually all estate plans minimize expenses after death. Not having a written plan ensures added costs and delay. Step #2 of this Guide provides a menu of estate planning goals so you can begin to set and prioritize your wishes, and then learn how to create an estate plan that embodies your goals.

GOAL: DON'T SPOIL THE KIDS

Let's face it: Unless you want to spoil your kids, 18 is not the best age for your children to inherit a lot of money. We often hear stories of children blowing their inheritance. In a 2011 U.S. Trust survey of 457 people with investable assets of more than $3 million, only 49% indicated it was important to leave an inheritance to their children Most parents, especially those with large estates, don't want their money squandered by the reckless exuberance of youth. Parents don't want spoiled, lazy kids. By transforming this philosophy into a goal, you can create an estate plan with ongoing trusts for children to help them become passionate, hard-working adults.

GOAL: HELP STRUGGLING CHILDREN

Sally had two children: a daughter who was financially successful and a son who struggled financially. Sally considered whether to leave more assets to her son than to her daughter—in other words, whether one of her goals was to help her struggling son.

Even when children are not struggling, some parents use their estate plan to equalize their children's wealth, leaving more to one child when another child is already well off. One real estate developer, for example, left more of his real estate to his middle child, who was not as well off as his other two children.

My parents considered implementing this goal into their estate plan. When my brother was better off financially than my sister and me, my dad asked me whether I thought that he and my mom should leave us more than my brother. After fighting the urge to respond "Absolutely!!" I practiced what I preach.

After explaining my conflict of interest in answering his question—after all, lawyers are always supposed to disclose a conflict of interest—I urged my father to think about his estate planning goals. Did he want to equalize the net worth of his children? He realized that he didn't want to use his estate plan to equalize our wealth. Instead, he wanted to treat all of us equally.

Talking about their goals also enabled my parents to think beyond the lives of their children. We talked about the transfer of wealth to their grandchildren. They realized that if they reduced my brother's share, his receiving less would penalize his four children.

Considering their estate planning goals also made them understand the huge emotional impact of their estate planning. How would my brother feel, and how would it impact my relationship with him, if my parents didn't treat us equally? After a long heart-to-heart, which is exactly the kind of discussion you should be having with your estate-planning attorney, my parents decided to keep their current estate plan, which distributes everything equally among the children in

an ongoing protected trust—something you'll learn more about in Step #3 of this 4-Step Action Guide.

GOAL: PUNISH CHILDREN

Some parents use an estate plan to express their hurt at a child's behavior, using the plan to punish the children. Gary, for example, was very angry with his daughter, who doesn't speak to him or allow him to see his grandchildren. He asked for my input on his inclination to leave all of his assets to his other two children and none to his "difficult" daughter.

I spoke with Gary about how his other two children would feel if their sister were left out of his estate plan, and how it would feel for his daughter, having just lost her father, to learn that she was disinherited. Ironically, his daughter was independently wealthy; her life would not materially change from not inheriting her father's assets, but emotionally it would likely affect her forever.

After we discussed love, life, and legacy, Gary decided he wanted to do anything he could to stop the family feuding. Gary told me he knew in his heart that disinheriting his daughter would only prolong family conflict, instead of ending it.

Gary hugged me when he signed his estate plan. Because he thought about his estate planning goals, he realized that disinheriting his difficult daughter was not consistent with his estate-planning goal of creating family harmony. Perhaps in death he could create the harmony that so far had eluded him in life.

Estate planning enables parents to think about what they want for their children. In fact, parents can use their estate plan to impact the lives of their children, grandchildren and future generations in a positive way.

GOAL: PROTECT KIDS IN THE EVENT OF DIVORCE

Studies reveal that 50% of first marriages end in divorce; that rate climbs to 60% for second, third, and later marriages. Whether you are happily married or divorced, you need to know how to ensure that a son-in-law or daughter-in-law only obtains possession of your assets if that is your intention, and not merely because of an unintended result of a failure to plan.

Some parents might not want to risk their assets ending up with a future son-in-law or daughter-in-law that they may not like. Others love their son/daughter in-law as much as their own child (sometimes more!) and plan their estate so that if their child is not living, the spouse gets everything.

Estate planning ensures that (1) the assets pass down to grandchildren and don't end up with a son-in-law or daughter-in-law or, conversely, (2) the in-laws are protected. Once you understand your goal, you will create the right estate plan tailored to achieve that goal.

GOAL: PROTECT HEIRS FROM SEXY SUE OR DON JUAN

Consider whether safeguarding your assets against a future second spouse is one of your estate planning goals. Many couples tell me that they trust each other 100%, and that they want their spouse to retain full control over <u>all</u> assets. Others want to make absolutely sure that their portion of the money goes to their children, and not to a second spouse. Once you set your goal, you can create an estate plan to implement it.

> *Oops—Nothing for the Kids:* At least several times a year, I see a client, a widowed man with a much younger woman, wanting to leave all of his assets to her. His primary estate-planning goal is to take care of his current wife, leaving her 100% of the assets (which would leave nothing for the kids), which I'm sure was not the estate planning goal of the first (now deceased) spouse.
>
> Had the man's first spouse insisted on an estate plan that prevented him from leaving her assets to a new spouse, the kids would have been protected. But often couples don't think about creating an estate plan that would protect the children. I envision the deceased first spouse stirring in her grave—such a sad thought about the realities of life, love and legacy.

Each spouse has a right to dispose of his or her portion of the assets (usually one-half of so-called "community property" assets in community property states like California). The couple's estate plan must address whether to allow the surviving spouse full control over the deceased spouse's assets. If you don't set clear goals, your children may find their inheritance going to their new stepparent.

GOAL: MAKE THE WORLD A BETTER PLACE

People often overlook charitable goals when preparing their estate plan. When I ask clients if they want to leave a gift to charity in their estate plan, they usually respond that they had not thought about it. Everyone should consider whether they want to include charitable giving in their estate plan. Otherwise, the support you have provided to charities during your lifetime will die with you.

Moreover, including charitable giving in your estate plan expresses your values. It sets an example for your children and highlights the value you place on charity and giving back. Your estate plan demonstrates your commitment to help others. When you include a charity in your estate plan, you leave a legacy that will last beyond your life.

As the Chair of the Legacy Circle at our Synagogue, I teach how easy it is to include charities in an estate plan. Often, the simplest and most tax efficient way to include charities in an estate plan is to name charities directly on the Beneficiary Designation form for a retirement account, such as an IRA. When you name *individuals* on a Beneficiary Designation for retirement accounts, they will be required to pay income tax on the distributions from the retirement account. However, when you name *charities* on the Beneficiary Designation, they will not be required to pay income tax on any distributions. Therefore, if you want both individuals and charities to benefit from your estate plan, consider leaving all of the assets in the Living Trust to the individuals, and all of the assets in the retirement accounts to the charities—assuming, of course, that the monetary values in each correspond with your goals.

People with a lot of money and charitable goals can sometimes minimize taxes by forming trusts for charity, which can be structured either to retain an income stream for themselves (called a Charitable Remainder Trust) or to give an income stream for a charity with the remainder going to children (called a Charitable Lead Trust). Using life insurance with the charitable trust can further enhance estate planning. Many organizations offer gift annuity programs in which you can make a donation in exchange for a lifetime annuity, which will provide a stream of income to you during your lifetime.

Many organizations also offer programs to recognize those who give to charity as part of their estate plan. Being recognized in the organization's "Legacy Circle" encourages those you leave behind to consider the charity's importance and impact. Your legacy gift sets an example for others. By spreading the word about charitable giving as part of an estate plan, we can help make the world a better place. See the Appendix for a simple Guide of Giving, listing a variety of easy ways to leave a legacy gift to charity.

My husband and I included our kids' high school in our estate plan. Coincidentally, the school includes the photo below of my dad and our son in their Legacy Society materials, which makes me feel proud every time I see the ad. Including the school in our estate plan hopefully encourages others to do the same. Together, one by one, we can make the world a better place by including charitable organizations in our estate plan.

The Legacy Society Materials From the High School Our Children Attended

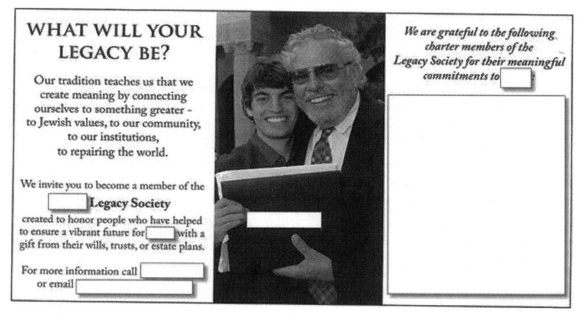

A STORY FROM THE TALMUD (Ta'anit 23a)

(Oral Jewish law written 2,500 years ago)
While walking along a road, a sage (named Choni) saw a man planting a carob tree. He asked him: "How long will it take for this tree to bear fruit?" "Seventy years," replied the man. The sage then asked: "Are you so healthy a man that you expect to live that length of time and eat its fruit?" The man answered: "I found a world containing carob trees, because my ancestors planted them for me. Likewise I am planting for my children."

MAKE THE WORLD A BETTER PLACE: THREE SIMPLE AND EASY WAYS TO LEAVE A MEANINGFUL LEGACY TO CHARITY

Including a charity in an estate plan helps ensure that the charity will thrive for children, grandchildren and many generations beyond. Sometimes people can't afford to donate a large amount during their lifetime, but at death they can use life insurance or retirement assets to make a huge difference.

Charitable giving that occurs upon death is referred to as **"Planned Giving,"** and comes in various forms:

❖ *Life insurance policy:* By naming a charitable organization on a short, simple form provided by the life insurance agent, the insurance will pass directly to the charitable organization without any court proceeding.

❖ *Retirement plan:* By naming a charitable organization on a short, simple form provided by the institution that holds an IRA, the retirement account will pass directly to the charitable organization without any court proceeding.

❖ *Will or Living Trust:* Simple language in a Will or Living Trust can instruct that assets be distributed to a charity. For example:
I give to _____, a charitable organization located at _____, whose tax ID number is_____, the sum of $_____ [or _____% of][or describe the real or personal property].

Call the charitable organization to ask for its legal name and Tax ID number. Most organizations can usually provide the proper language to give assets to an endowment fund, which allows the gift to be held and invested for years after your demise. Endowments make a difference. Each year, an endowment will make a distribution of a portion of your gift to support the charity. The endowment provides regular annual funding, even after death, to support a cause you believe in.

Talk to your legal/tax advisor about what is best for you. It is fun and meaningful to create an estate plan that embodies your ethics.

GOAL: MINIMIZE TAX UNDER CURRENT LAW

In 1789, when Benjamin Franklin wrote, "In this world nothing can be certain, except death and taxes," he hadn't read the Taxpayer Relief Act. Although death is still certain (hopefully after a long, full life), taxes are not—at least not estate tax. The Taxpayer Relief Act helps eliminate Federal estate tax for the majority of people. (See Step #3 of this Guide, Estate Planning Boot Camp, to learn how the Taxpayer Relief Act affects your estate plan.)

In fact, the amount that can be left free of estate tax ($5,340,000 in 2014) has more than quadrupled since 2001. Further, according to the Urban-Brookings Tax Policy Center, less than 2 out of every 1,000 people who die owe any estate tax. In other words, 99.86% of those dying pay no Federal estate tax. While Benjamin Franklin was right that everybody dies, he was wrong about Federal estate taxes—currently paid only by the very wealthy.

While reducing Federal estate tax won't be the number one goal of most people (because the law does that already), residents of states with a state inheritance tax and those with real property in such states need to address their state's estate tax laws. Further, most people will want to reduce other types of taxes, like income and property tax.

As certain tax deductions are phased out and some taxes increased (including the net investment income "surtax" of the Obama administration), estate plans need to be established or updated to minimize *income* tax. Without setting income tax planning as a goal, beneficiaries will likely pay income tax that could have been avoided with proper planning. Outdated estate plans created before the Taxpayer Relief Act can cause disaster today:

> *The Income Tax Nightmare:* Amanda and Craig should have been more concerned about *income tax* than estate tax. They had an $800,000 home and $400,000 in the bank. The Living Trust they created in 2008, which focused on reducing estate tax, turned into an income tax nightmare when Craig died from cancer. Unfortunately, they never reassessed their estate planning goals after passage of the Taxpayer Relief Act.

> Amanda and Craig no longer needed an estate plan to minimize estate tax because the Taxpayer Relief Act already exempted their assets from estate tax. Their $1.2M estate was far below what they could leave free of estate tax. Without additional costly planning, their Living Trust, which required setting up complicated trusts that were designed to reduce estate tax, will increase income tax on the assets transferred into the now obsolete trusts.

ATTENTION: CRITICAL INFORMATION FOR CALIFORNIA RESIDENTS OR OWNERS OF CALIFORNIA REAL PROPERTY Avoiding property tax increases after a death is a critical goal for owners of California real property with low property taxes thanks to Proposition 13. Death creates a so-called "change of ownership," meaning that property taxes will be reassessed to the fair market value at the date of death, unless a so-called "exclusion" from reassessment applies. With proper planning, you can help ensure that your family can afford to keep your real property.

Discover and Set Your Estate Planning Goals, Before It's Too Late

Setting your goals will determine both the timing and the structure of your estate plan. Studies show that the process of writing down a goal increases your chances of reaching that goal. Write down a date, no later than 30 days from today, by which your plan will be complete.

Now reflect on your life. Have some fun with this. Estate planning should make you feel good. What have you created in your life so far? What are you most proud of? Take into account whether you have parents to support, or a challenging child. Consider the charitable organizations that you've supported during your lifetime and whether you want to provide for them in your estate plan. Do you have a child who is disabled or receives (or could receive) needs-based public assistance such as SSI? Think about the people reading your estate plan and what your estate plan will tell them about you. Consider whether you want your plan to encourage your children to have a strong work ethic. What would you hope for after you are no longer living?

Don't skip this step or say that you will do it later. By reading this book, you have decided to act now and get your affairs in order. Review the list of possible estate planning goals below, check the ones that resonate with you, add your own unique goals and bring this list when you meet with your estate planning attorney for a more focused, productive and successful meeting. After all, you want your estate plan to be a reflection of your life and your goals.

ESTATE PLANNING GOALS:

_____   Get organized

_____   Minimize legal fees

_____   Reduce expenses at death

_____   Keep things simple

_____   Minimize court costs

_____   Minimize estate tax

_____   Avoid property tax increase

_____   Ensure assets go to children

_____   Designate assets for education

_____   Protect kids' work ethic so they don't get spoiled

_____   Preserve a child's public benefits

_____   Avoid conflict between kids and a second spouse

_____   Protect assets for kids in case spouse re-marries

_____   Ensure son-in-law or daughter-in-law receives assets

_____   Protect assets from a son-in-law or daughter-in-law

_____   Disinherit a particular person

_____   Avoid family conflict

_____   Transfer wealth to existing grandchildren

_____   Protect assets for (future) grandchildren

_____   Protect assets from creditors

_____   Provide for spouse

_____   Provide for a spouse from a second marriage

_____   Donate to charities

_____   Plan for business succession

_____   Leave money to a caregiver

OTHER NOTES/THOUGHTS/GOALS:

_____

_____

_____

_____

_____

_____

_____

_____

_____

_____

_____

_____

_____

_____

_____

_____

THE TAKE-AWAY FROM STEP #2

Even if you already have an estate plan, it is vital to pull it out of the drawer and take another look. The plan you created in the past may not work for you now. Your goals from 2001 may be different from your estate planning goals today. By taking Step #2, you can evaluate your current estate planning goals.

We all have unique goals. One-size-fits-all estate plans do not work. The wealthy may need a plan to reduce estate tax. A young woman with a terminally ill spouse may also need to plan to minimize estate tax, but for different reasons: She will probably live much longer than her husband, during which time her assets will increase in value. Couples with children may want a plan to protect the kids' inheritance from an unknown future spouse. Business owners may need a plan for business succession. A parent of a special needs child may need to plan for maintaining the child's public benefits. Establish your goals now. Then proceed to Step #3, Estate Planning Boot Camp, which will teach you all you need to know and answer the questions you didn't know to ask.

ESTATE PLANNING BOOT CAMP: WHAT EVERYBODY MUST KNOW

From 2001 to 2013, estate-planning laws changed so drastically from year to year that many people were afraid to prepare a plan, thinking it would become obsolete almost immediately.

From 2001 to 2013, estate-planning laws changed so drastically from year to year that many people were afraid to prepare a plan, thinking it would become obsolete almost immediately. When the "permanent" estate tax law under the Taxpayer Relief Act became effective in 2013, people started to think again about estate planning. However, confusion about the current law can stymie the process. Turning to the internet and its enormous amount of information (and misinformation) can lead to more confusion and paralysis. And then it's too late.

> *Analysis Paralysis:* Diane, whom we discussed earlier, was so confused about her estate plan that she never finished it. Even though several trust drafts were created, her analysis paralysis prevented her from completing the process. After she died, $80,000 of her money went to attorneys, the courts and the court-appointed administrator, and the balance went to distant relatives she never met.

In the Estate Planning Boot Camp below, you will learn the 14 Critical Facts that are essential to making a fully informed decision about your estate planning. Then,

in Step #4, you can evaluate whether you want to hire an attorney to complete your plan or do it yourself, and get it done!

Critical Fact #1: The Anatomy of an Estate Plan and the Terminology You MUST Know

Estate planning might feel like a foreign language, but in fact it's relatively easy. Understanding a few concepts enables you to determine your goals, how to achieve them, and how to discuss them with a professional or your family.

THE FIVE ESSENTIAL DOCUMENTS OF MOST ESTATE PLANS

Most estate plans require five essential documents:

❖ A **Living Trust** is an instruction manual explaining who's in charge of your assets when you can't manage them and who gets what when you die. It's like a Will that you can change at any time (assuming you have capacity), except your assets are re-titled into a Living Trust. Also, unlike a Will, a funded Living Trust will avoid costly court proceedings if you die or are incapacitated. You are the "**settlor**," meaning the person creating the trust. You can amend or revoke your Living Trust during your lifetime, unless you lack "**capacity**," a legal standard that will determine whether your revocation or amendment is legally valid. A Living Trust is sometimes called a "**revocable trust**" because you can change it as long as you have mental capacity and testamentary capacity (i.e., someone in a coma would not have the capacity to change a trust).

Typically, when you create a Living Trust, you will also be the initial "**Trustee**," the person in charge of the assets. The Trustee you name in the trust to succeed you, sometimes called a successor Trustee, will take charge of your assets when you can't.

If you create a Living Trust when you are experiencing difficulty handling your finances, perhaps you are older or have health issues, consider whether you want to name someone other than yourself as the initial Trustee of the Living Trust. Parents sometimes name a trusted child or a professional fiduciary to be the initial Trustee and retain the power to remove and replace the Trustee. Of course, think carefully before giving up this control and make sure you completely trust the Trustee that you are appointing.

After your demise, the Trustee you name to succeed you will distribute the assets to "**beneficiaries**," the people and charitable organizations named in your Living Trust to receive your assets, not to be confused with the person or institution you appoint to manage and distribute your assets to the beneficiaries, which is called the Trustee. Often a Living Trust will instruct the Trustee to continue holding assets for the beneficiaries. For example, assets might be held in a "**Dynasty Trust**" after your demise, meaning that the trust will continue for the entire lifetime of the children and then pass to their children. Parents with young children should always include an ongoing trust in their Living Trust, instructing the Trustee to safeguard the money and property until the children are at least 25 years old.

A Living Trust is not a separate taxpaying entity, and therefore the trust uses the social security number of the creator rather than a separate tax ID number.

> **ATTENTION OWNERS OF CALIFORNIA PROPERTY** Very importantly, when California real property is transferred into a Living Trust, property taxes will not be reassessed.

LIFE LESSONS:

In the song Dark Horse off her Prism album, Katy Perry sings "you better choose carefully." This couldn't be truer than in estate planning. Choosing a Trustee is one of the most important estate planning decision you will make. Name someone trustworthy, with good business judgment and strong organization skills, at ease and savvy in dealing with attorneys and accountants, and who shares your values. Choosing the wrong Trustee for your Living Trust can be disastrous. The Trustee appointed by one couple held a garage sale of all the precious family belongings without giving notice to the adult children. Any legal recourse the kids had after the garage sale was too little too late!

Be cautious about appointing your children as Trustee of your Living Trust. If children do not get along, the bickering will not end with your death. Appointing a trusted neutral party as the Trustee of the Living Trust can go a long way toward creating peace in the family.

❖ A **Will** specifies who gets what when you die. If you have a Living Trust, your Will is known as a "**Pour Over Will**" because it provides

for your assets not already titled in the Living Trust to pour over into your Living Trust after death. In the Will, you appoint an **"executor"** who will handle the administration in probate court, a **"guardian of the person"** to care for your minor children (assuming both parents are deceased), and a **"guardian of the estate"** to control your minor children's assets.

Unlike a Living Trust, a Will does not authorize anyone to manage your assets if you become incapacitated. Therefore, if you can't manage your own assets while you are living, the court may handle matters in a proceeding called a **"conservatorship."** To avoid probate court at death and a conservatorship during your life, consider creating a Living Trust, transferring your assets to the Living Trust and creating a Pour Over Will to ensure that all your assets will be transferred to your Living Trust when you die.

LIFE LESSONS:

People often appoint a guardian in a Will without specifying whether the person is supposed to act as the "guardian of the estate" or the "guardian of the person." The person caring for the children might be awful handling money. Be sure your Will appoints the right person as the caretaker and the right person to handle the money. Often, the guardian of the estate will be the same person you named as the Trustee of the Living Trust—the same person with a different title.

❖ The **Durable Power of Attorney** allows you to appoint someone in the event of your incapacity, called an **"attorney-in-fact,"** to manage assets that are not titled in the Living Trust. The Durable Power of Attorney pertains to your retirement accounts and any other assets that you hold outside of your trust. Typically, you will appoint the same person to act as Trustee under the Living Trust as the attorney-in-fact under the Durable Power of Attorney because this person will handle your assets.

LIFE LESSONS:

More and more institutions require their own durable power of attorney forms. For any retirement account, be sure to contact the institution that holds the account and complete its durable power of attorney form so that someone will be able to stand in your shoes to manage it (i.e., the investments or arranging for required minimum distributions) if you become incapacitated.

❖ The **Health Care Directive** allows you to appoint an "**agent**" to make your health care decisions when you are incapacitated. A release known as an **Authorization to Disclose and Release Protected Health Information**[1] allows your physician to release protected health care information to your successor Trustee of the Living Trust and agent under the Health Care Directive.

❖ **Written Instructions for Distribution of Tangible Personal Property** instructs the Trustee of the Living Trust (or the executor of the Will) to distribute your personal property—such as jewelry, furniture, art and family heirlooms—to named individuals. The Written Instructions typically will only control the distribution of your personal property if you include a corresponding provision in your Living Trust or Will that authorizes the Trustee or executor to rely on the Written Instructions.

LIFE LESSONS:

Families fight over personal property as much if not more than over huge bank accounts. Inserting provisions in a Living Trust or Will that allows the use of separate, detailed written instructions about distributing personal property after death can save a lot of grief for your family. Your family will thank you. Think about what family heirlooms are likely to create conflict and include specific instructions in your estate plan. By including your instructions on a separate signed and notarized document, you can easily change it without needing a full-blown amendment to your Living Trust or Will.

❖ The **Certification of Trust** is a relatively short summary of the Living Trust, which includes the legal name of the Living Trust, the date signed, the Trustee powers and instructions on how to take title of assets in the Living Trust. You will present a copy of the Certification of Trust to banks and title companies to show them exactly how you want to take title to your assets.

LIFE LESSONS:

Attach a copy of the first and last pages of the Living Trust and the pages with the Trustee powers to the Certification of Trust. If you scan it and keep it on your computer in PDF format, you can easily e-mail or print it for whoever may need it (i.e., the escrow officer when you are buying property, or the bank when you are opening a bank account).

LIVING TRUSTS COME IN ALL SIZES AND SHAPES, JUST LIKE THE PEOPLE WHO CREATE THEM

While a Living Trust is one of the five basic documents of an estate plan, the Living Trust can create within it other trusts that won't be funded with assets until after a death. Understanding the trusts that can be funded after a death will help you create an estate plan tailored to your needs and unique circumstances.

Trusts funded after a death are ongoing trusts sometimes referred to as **"Irrevocable Trusts"** when the ongoing trusts cannot be revoked (without jumping through some hoops). For example, parents might provide in their Living Trust that when the last parent dies, the assets are to be held in an ongoing Irrevocable Trust for their children until they reach the age of 25. An Irrevocable Trust for the children could be a **"Dynasty Trust,"** meaning that it lasts for more than one generation, providing significant protection for children and grandchildren.

Before the Taxpayer Relief Act, most married couples included Irrevocable Trusts within their Living Trust. For example, a traditional Living Trust (sometimes referred to as an **ABC Living Trust)** provides that when one spouse dies, the assets get transferred into ongoing Trusts, sometimes called Trust A, Trust B and Trust C.

Couples traditionally use an ABC Living Trust to ensure that the assets of the deceased spouse are transferred to the children when the surviving spouse dies and to protect the assets from being taken by creditors (for example if the surviving spouse were involved in a lawsuit). Before the Taxpayer Relief Act, when relatively little could pass free of estate tax, couples also needed to create complicated ongoing trusts to minimize estate tax. The legal names of the ongoing Trusts created under an ABC Living Trust are the **Survivor's Trust, Bypass Trust** and **QTIP Trust**, as further explained below.

❖ **Survivor's Trust**: All of the surviving spouse's trust assets will fund a Survivor's Trust, an ongoing, fully flexible trust created by an ABC Living Trust after one spouse dies. The surviving spouse maintains full and absolute control over all the assets that are funded into the Survivor's Trust. The Survivor's Trust is a Revocable Trust, meaning that the surviving spouse can change the terms of the Survivor's Trust and leave those assets to anyone the survivor wants. In a community property state, such as Arizona, California, Idaho, Louisiana, Nevada, New Mexico, Texas, Washington, and Wisconsin, typically one-half of the trust assets will be funded into the Survivor's Trust when one spouse dies.

❖ **Bypass Trust and QTIP Trust**: All of a deceased spouse's trust assets will fund a Bypass Trust and a QTIP Trust, sometimes informally referred to as Trust B and Trust C under an ABC Living Trust. The assets that the deceased spouse can leave free of estate tax because of that spouse's remaining "Exemption" get transferred into the Bypass Trust when one spouse dies. The Exemption refers to the maximum that can be left at death or gifted during life free of transfer tax. The deceased spouse's assets valued over the Exemption get transferred into the QTIP Trust. The trust can be drafted to allow the surviving spouse access to all the assets in the Bypass Trust and the QTIP Trust for the surviving spouse's support. Placing assets in both the Bypass Trust and QTIP trust protects the assets from creditors and second spouses, and the assets in the Bypass Trust, *including all appreciation,* when properly administered, will not be subject to estate tax <u>when the surviving spouse dies.</u> Think of the Bypass Trust and QTIP Trust as insurance that the remaining assets will pass to the children while minimizing estate tax.

❖ **The "All to Spouse Plan with Optional Disclaimer Trust"**: With the passage of the Taxpayer Relief Act, more married couples will create a simple Living Trust, rather than an ABC Living Trust. This 4-Step Action Guide refers to the simplest type of Living Trust for a married couple as the "All to Spouse Plan with Optional Disclaimer Trust." The "All to Spouse Plan" provisions of this type of Living Trust leave *all* the trust assets in a Revocable Trust, an ongoing, flexible trust for the surviving spouse, giving the surviving spouse full control over all of the assets, including the power to leave the assets to whomever the surviving spouse wants. The "Optional Disclaimer Trust" provisions give the

ATTENTION WOMEN: According to Howard S. Friedman and Leslie R. Martin, co-authors of *The Longevity Project: Surprising Discoveries for Health and Long Life* from the Landmark Eight-Decade Study, women on average live seven years longer than men. So understand how ongoing trusts will impact you, your assets and your life. Make sure that your Living Trust meets your needs.

surviving spouse the option to decline accepting some of the assets, which the surviving spouse might do to minimize estate tax when she dies or to protect the assets from potential creditors. For example, if the surviving spouse were worried that her assets might be so significant that they might be subject to estate tax when she dies (i.e., they might be more than her available Exemption from estate tax), she might sign a document called a **"qualified disclaimer,"** indicating that she does not want some of the trust assets. In addition to other requirements, the qualified disclaimer must be signed and delivered to the Trustee of the Living Trust within nine months of her husband's death.

If the surviving spouse follows all the rules to create a qualified disclaimer, the Trustee of the Living Trust would then distribute the disclaimed assets to an ongoing Irrevocable Trust, known as the **Disclaimer Trust**. The assets disclaimed would be re-titled into the Disclaimer Trust, and would be available to the surviving spouse for her support. Much like a Bypass Trust that passes free of estate tax when the surviving spouse dies, the Disclaimer Trust, when properly administered, protects assets, including all appreciation, from estate tax when the surviving spouse dies. The assets in the Disclaimer Trust pass to the beneficiary (usually the children) exactly as indicated in the Living Trust, without any power of the surviving spouse to change anything. The Option to Disclaim is like giving the surviving spouse the power to create a Bypass Trust, but rather than having to make that decision when both spouses are living, she can wait nine months after her husband dies. Considering how many things can change from the time a Living Trust is created to when a spouse actually dies, the All to Spouse Plan with Optional Disclaimer Trust allows many couples to make a better, more informed decision than the ABC Trust, which locks the surviving spouse into forming Irrevocable Trusts after one spouse dies. However, unlike the Bypass Trust, once the surviving spouse completes the qualified disclaimer, she can't change the final beneficiaries of the trust. For example, if she has a falling out with one child, the surviving spouse would not be able to leave that child's share to her other children or to her grandchildren.

Critical Fact #2: The Taxpayer Relief Act Has Changed the Role of Living Trusts

THE NEW ERA OF ESTATE PLANNING: WHAT'S CHANGED

Now that we have explored some basic estate planning concepts, we turn to the Taxpayer Relief Act – its consequences, how it can adversely affect you and what you need to do about it. The Taxpayer Relief Act has revolutionized estate planning. Understanding how the law affects you will help you determine what action you need to take to avoid the law's potentially negative consequences.

In 1983, when I first became a lawyer, transfers over $275,000 were subject to a transfer tax, meaning a "gift tax" for assets transferred during life and an "estate tax" upon a death, and the highest tax rate was 60%, so most people needed an estate plan to minimize estate tax at death. Married couples would create a Living Trust that provided for the deceased spouse's Exemption amount to be transferred into an Irrevocable Trust called a Bypass Trust, allowing the assets to pass free of estate tax when the surviving spouse later died.

Unlike prior estate tax law, which kept changing every year, the current law is "permanent" in that there is no set expiration date—the tax rate and the Exemption amount that can pass free of transfer tax stay the same each year, except for annual cost of living adjustments. The Taxpayer Relief Act now simplifies the ability to minimize *estate tax* for about 99% of the population. Because most people don't have millions of dollars, they no longer have to worry about estate tax. But keep reading! Even if you're part of that 99%, you still need a well-crafted estate plan to focus on all your other *non-estate tax* goals. (Read the many horror stories sprinkled throughout this book to remind yourself of the dire consequences if you fail to create an estate plan.)

THREE BIG CHANGES TO ESTATE PLANNING

Under the current law, you can now take the necessary action to protect your family and safeguard your assets—as long as you understand the three biggest changes created by the Taxpayer Relief Act and how it affects your estate plan.

1. EXEMPTION IS HIGHER: You can now transfer more assets without transfer tax. Under the current law, $5 million, plus an amount indexed annually for inflation, passes "exempt" or free from transfer tax. With

New Law: The Past and Present of Portability
The Unemployment Insurance Reauthorization and Job Creation Act of 2010 introduced something revolutionary for married couples: "portability." The new but temporary 2-year law allowed one spouse to carry over the unused estate tax exclusion amount, or Exemption, to a surviving spouse. Portability offered couples the potential for two Exemptions—the survivor's Exemption and the deceased spouse's Exemption—without the necessity of working with an attorney or creating complicated trusts. But couples couldn't rely on portability because the original law expired on December 31, 2012.

The American Taxpayer Relief Act of 2012, which went into effect in January 2013, eliminated all the uncertainty: The ability to "port" the Exemption from a deceased spouse to the surviving spouse was called "permanent," as was the Exemption amount of $5 million with annual cost of living increases, in that the law had no set expiration date.

the indexed increase, a U.S. citizen or resident can gift $5.34 million in 2014 (or die with that amount) free of transfer tax.

2. FLAT TRANSFER TAX RATE IS LOWER: Each dollar over the Exemption that is either gifted during life or left at death is now taxed at a flat rate of 40%—a decrease from the 55% maximum tax rate of prior years. While *income tax* rates have been increasing, *estate tax* rates have been decreasing.

3. EXEMPTION OF ONE SPOUSE IS PORTABLE TO THE SURVIVING SPOUSE: Portability allows couples to use each other's unused Exemption without having to create complicated trusts. Unlike the prior "use it or lose it" rule, a spouse who dies with assets under the Exemption can now port, or transfer, the unused Exemption to the surviving spouse if the surviving spouse files a timely estate tax return electing portability, and if certain other criteria are met.

For example, if one spouse has $2 million of assets and never made any lifetime gifts that used his Exemption, under 2014 law that spouse won't use all of his Exemption. Of the $5.34 million Exemption, for example, he will have $3.34 million of unused Exemption ($5.34 million minus $2 million).

The $3.34 million of unused Exemption can be ported to the surviving spouse. If ported, the surviving spouse potentially can use her own Exemption PLUS the Exemption that the deceased spouse did not use, so long as the surviving spouse dies with the deceased spouse as her last spouse (meaning that the surviving spouse didn't re-marry someone who also predeceased her) and certain other criteria are met. Great news: The surviving spouse could then transfer her Exemption plus her deceased spouse's $3.34 million of unused Exemption free of transfer tax, opening the gateway to some very creative planning!

Before portability, the surviving spouse needed to fund an Irrevocable Trust (i.e., a Bypass Trust or a Disclaimer Trust) to retain the benefit of the assets and the deceased spouse's Exemption. Further, before portability, generally only assets funded into the Bypass Trust or Disclaimer Trust were protected, not assets that passed to the surviving spouse outside of the Living Trust (unless the couple had a Spousal Property Agreement). Portability now enables the surviving spouse to capture the tax benefit of the deceased spouse's Exemption without funding Irrevocable Trusts that require ongoing annual tax returns and administration. For most couples, estate planning has become simpler, as long as they understand the concepts in this 4-Step Action Guide!

SHIFT OF FOCUS AWAY FROM ESTATE TAX AVOIDANCE

Although a Living Trust is still critical to avoid probate court, Living Trusts appropriately crafted before the Taxpayer Relief Act to decrease estate tax may increase another type of tax—income tax. Therefore, not all Living Trusts should be drafted to minimize estate tax. Essentially, under current law—with the higher Exemption, lower estate tax rates, and portability of the Exemption—people can transfer more wealth transfer tax-free without a Living Trust that requires assets to be funded after death in Irrevocable Trusts like the Bypass Trust.

Thus, after the Taxpayer Relief Act, some couples must focus less on estate tax and more on income tax (including capital gains tax), property tax and safeguarding assets for children—as I explain fully below. In Critical Fact #4, I discuss the pitfalls of relying solely on portability, why you still may want your Living Trust to create an Irrevocable Trust after the first spouse dies, and other options you should consider to avoid the adverse income tax consequences of traditional Bypass Trusts that were drafted in the era before the Taxpayer Relief Act.

Critical Fact #3: Consider Bypassing the Traditional Bypass Trust and Choose Better Options

THE SHIFTING ROLE OF THE BYPASS TRUST

For many married couples, a Living Trust created properly before the Taxpayer Relief Act will result in more money than necessary going to the IRS and less to their family. In prior years (like 1983, when the IRS taxed everything over $275,000 at death, and 1987, when the IRS taxed everything over $600,000), Living Trusts typically instructed the Trustee to transfer assets into a Bypass Trust after the death of the first spouse. Although a Bypass Trust would have saved estate tax under pre-Taxpayer Relief Act laws, this type of trust may no longer be necessary to minimize estate tax, and it may in fact increase income tax!

The Bypass Trust that Didn't Bypass Taxes: A recently widowed woman came to meet with me. Even though she and her deceased husband only possessed a $400,000 home and $400,000 in the bank for a total estate of $800,000, their ABC Living Trust required the Trustee to put her deceased husband's assets into a Bypass Trust.

Her hands were tied—even though she and her husband had far less than what could pass estate tax free under the Exemption, $400,000 of assets needed to be funded into an Irrevocable Trust that required ongoing trust administration. Even worse, funding her house or bank account into an Irrevocable Trust would probably increase *income tax* after she dies.

Assume, for example, that the $400,000 house was funded into the Irrevocable Bypass Trust, and she lives for another 30 years. If the house triples in value to $1,200,000, in 30 years, when the children sell the house, they will be required to pay income tax on the entire gain. If we assume an income tax rate of 28%, the children will be paying $336,000 in income taxes.

The unfortunate outcome would be that the funding of the Bypass Trust didn't save any estate tax because under current law, the surviving spouse could leave over $5 million without paying any estate tax even without the Bypass Trust. However, putting assets into the Bypass Trust increased *income tax* by over $300,000.

Over the years, as the Exemption increased from $275,000 to $5 million, married couples kept Bypass Trusts provisions to minimize estate tax, fearing that the Exemption would revert to $1 million, as provided under the pre-Taxpayer Relief Act. Because the Exemption amount was temporary, married couples continued to position the Bypass Trust as the cornerstone of their Living Trust, believing that minimizing estate tax if the Exemption were lowered would outweigh the income tax hit from the Bypass Trust.

With the Exemption now higher and portable, married couples should evaluate whether to bypass the Bypass Trust. If the Bypass Trust does not save estate tax, but potentially increases income tax, married couples may want to steer clear.

In addition, rising income tax rates are changing the focus of estate planning. In California, Proposition 30, approved by voters in November 2012, increased state income tax through 2018, making California's top income tax rate the highest of any state in the nation. Long term capital gains tax rates have also climbed. Rather than focusing on estate tax, most people should focus on estate planning strategies to minimize income tax.

THE DEVIL'S IN THE DETAILS; A DEEPER LOOK INTO THE BYPASS TRUST—THE GOOD, THE BAD AND THE UGLY

Because the current high estate tax Exemption has no set expiration date, married couples need to gain a deeper understanding of Bypass Trusts to determine whether to include one in their Living Trust. What are the other options? Should the surviving spouse file an estate tax return after the death of the first spouse and elect portability as an alternative to the Bypass Trust? The following discussion will enable couples to make the right decision when planning their estate.

The good news about Bypass Trusts: In addition to being harder for creditors to reach, all assets transferred into the Bypass Trust when one spouse dies, *including any increase in value from the date of the first spouse's death until the surviving spouse's death*, will avoid all estate tax when the <u>surviving spouse</u> dies.

Critical Action Steps for Married Couples Couples with ABC Living Trusts MUST review and assess their goals to determine whether they want or need a traditional Bypass Trust and whether provisions should be added so that the Bypass Trust can be converted into a QTIP-Protection Trust. Surviving spouses with assets already funded into an Irrevocable Bypass Trust should consider taking a distribution so that, upon their death, the assets are not in the Bypass Trust. After a death, surviving spouses with ABC Living Trusts should also talk to their advisor about seeking a court order to terminate the Bypass Trust. Alternatively, the surviving spouse could consider funding the Bypass Trust with a promissory note rather than with trust assets.

In effect, the assets transferred into the Bypass Trust are grandfathered in and can grow an unlimited amount without being subject to estate tax when the surviving spouse dies. Even if the Exemption is lower than the value of the Bypass Trust assets, all the assets pass *estate tax* free!

The surviving spouse can also maintain tremendous control over the assets in the Bypass Trust. The assets can be used by the surviving spouse for support and can be sold and re-invested at the discretion of the surviving spouse, assuming she is appointed Trustee. Better yet, the spouse who dies first has the peace of mind knowing that the beneficiaries named in the Living Trust will get the remaining funds in the Bypass Trust, not a new spouse (who might be a floozy!).

The bad news about Bypass Trusts: Although all Bypass Trust assets pass to the named beneficiaries free of estate tax, when appreciated assets in the Bypass Trust are sold after the surviving spouse dies, the remainder beneficiaries typically will pay income tax (capital gains tax) on all the gain. For example, if the $5.34 million of assets put into the Bypass Trust appreciated to $7.34 million during the surviving spouse's lifetime, the beneficiaries will pay capital gains tax on the $2 million of gain when the beneficiaries sell those assets after the surviving spouse dies.

Had all the assets been distributed to the surviving spouse and not to the Bypass Trust, the beneficiaries could have avoided all capital gains tax. Putting assets into the Bypass Trust resulted in more tax, not less, because the beneficiaries will pay capital gains tax when they sell appreciated assets in the Bypass Trust after the surviving spouse dies.

And the ugly: The bad news gets even worse if the surviving spouse would have had enough Exemption to shelter all the assets without the Bypass Trust. For example, if the couple did not need to fund the Bypass Trust to save estate tax, but doing so resulted in higher income tax, the beneficiaries are not going to be happy campers. In this new era of estate planning post Taxpayer Relief Act, because couples can port the unused Exemption, the Bypass Trust may not minimize estate tax but may increase *income tax*. That's pretty ugly!

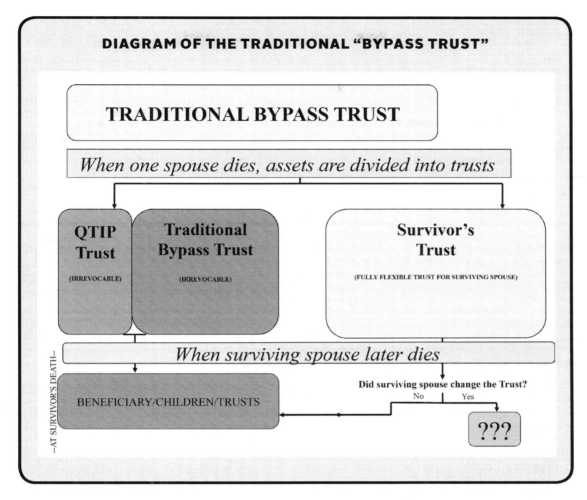

DIAGRAM OF THE TRADITIONAL "BYPASS TRUST"

TRADITIONAL BYPASS TRUST

When one spouse dies, assets are divided into trusts

QTIP Trust
(IRREVOCABLE)

Traditional Bypass Trust
(IRREVOCABLE)

Survivor's Trust
(FULLY FLEXIBLE TRUST FOR SURVIVING SPOUSE)

When surviving spouse later dies

–AT SURVIVOR'S DEATH–

BENEFICIARY/CHILDREN/TRUSTS

Did surviving spouse change the Trust?
No   Yes

???

Now that we've covered the good, the bad and the ugly of the Bypass Trust, let's explore another type of Living Trust, the stepsister of the Bypass Trust.

The Stepsister Becomes Cinderella; the "All to Spouse Plan with Optional Disclaimer Trust"—a Flexible Alternative to the Bypass Trust
Unlike the Living Trust that *requires* the Trustee to fund assets into an Irrevocable Bypass Trust, some Living Trusts offer the surviving spouse the *option* to fund an Irrevocable Trust. The "All to Spouse Plan with Optional Disclaimer Trust" allows the surviving spouse to do just that.

The Living Trust with an "All to Spouse Plan" instructs the Trustee to transfer all the assets to the surviving spouse, providing her an option that would allow the Trustee to fund some or all of the deceased spouse's assets into an Irrevocable Trust. The Trustee would then fund assets into an Irrevocable Disclaimer Trust rather than an Irrevocable Bypass Trust. While the Bypass Trust and her stepsister Disclaimer

Trust both protect assets, the Bypass Trust must be funded, while funding of the Disclaimer Trust is optional, allowing the surviving spouse to wait and see.

To exercise the option to disclaim under the All to Spouse Plan with Optional Disclaimer Trust, the surviving spouse needs to follow certain rules, including signing a written document, referred to as a Qualified Disclaimer[2], within nine months after the death of the first spouse and before receiving any benefit of the assets being disclaimed. If the surviving spouse wants the estate tax or creditor protection of a trust similar to the Bypass Trust, the surviving spouse would disclaim some or all of the assets of the deceased spouse. Then, those assets disclaimed would be re-titled into an Irrevocable Trust called a Disclaimer Trust, while those assets not disclaimed would be held in a very flexible ongoing trust. Both trusts will benefit the surviving spouse, but the Disclaimer Trust is designed to protect the assets from creditors and to allow the assets to pass free of estate tax when the surviving spouse dies.

Like a Bypass Trust, the assets in the Disclaimer Trust *and all appreciation on those assets* pass free of estate tax when the surviving spouse dies. On the downside, like the Bypass Trust, the Disclaimer Trust will require annual accountings (unless waived) and tax returns. More significantly, as with the Bypass Trust, putting assets in the Disclaimer Trust will usually subject appreciated assets to capital gains tax upon sale after the surviving spouse dies.

While couples use the Bypass Trust for *pre-death planning* (the Living Trust mandates transfer of the deceased spouse's assets valued up to the unused Exemption into the Bypass Trust), couples use the All to Spouse Plan with Optional Disclaimer Trust for *post-death planning* (the surviving spouse decides whether and how much to disclaim, which the Trustee will then place into the Disclaimer Trust). Similar to the Bypass Trust, the Disclaimer Trust:

- ❖ Protects assets from estate tax, irrespective whether the surviving spouse remarries.
- ❖ Allows assets to grow in value without being subject to estate tax.
- ❖ Allows assets to transfer to grandchildren transfer-tax free.
- ❖ Protects assets from creditors.

The All to Spouse Plan with an Optional Disclaimer Trust is superior to the Bypass Trust *in certain situations* because it gives the surviving spouse more flexibility. The surviving spouse makes the decision after one spouse dies, not while drafting the estate plan. Unless the surviving spouse disclaims, he or she doesn't have to file separate tax returns every year, which means he or she has very little reporting and administrative burdens while still being able to use the assets for support.

> *I Hate Paperwork:* One woman in her seventies with an ill husband wanted one thing above all else: simplicity. She wanted the simplest plan possible so that when her husband died, she would not be over-whelmed with paperwork. She did not want to deal with separate tax ID numbers for various trusts followed by the ongoing administra-tion of those trusts. They created a simple Living Trust leaving all their assets to the surviving spouse, giving her an option to fund an Irrevocable Disclaimer Trust.

Before giving it a standing ovation, understand the downside of the All to Spouse Plan with Optional Disclaimer Trust—the spouse who dies first loses all control; the surviving spouse can leave all the assets to a new spouse, unless the surviv-ing spouse disclaims. Further, if the surviving spouse disclaims assets, she can't even make minor changes to the beneficiary list. The surviving spouse can use the assets in the Disclaimer Trust for support, but has zero ability to change the final distribution of the remaining assets.

Instructions in the Living Trust, which may have been written 20 years before the surviving spouse dies, will control what happens. If a child becomes addicted to drugs, for example, the surviving spouse would not be able to remove the child from the Disclaimer Trust. If a child becomes irresponsible or gets divorced, the surviving spouse cannot revise the terms of any trust that may have been created for that child. In other words, the surviving spouse who disclaims cannot decide who gets the assets after the survivor dies.

The surviving spouse would only disclaim after determining that the potential estate tax and creditor protection benefits of the Disclaimer Trust will offset the disadvan-tages: the need to file annual tax returns and produce periodic accountings, the poten-tial capital gains tax on the sale of appreciated assets after the surviving spouse's death, and the inability to tweak the final distribution of the Disclaimer Trust assets. The All to Spouse Plan with Optional Disclaimer Trust allows the surviving spouse to weigh the pros and the cons of getting all the assets versus disclaiming, making an informed decision in light of the facts and circumstances after the death of the first spouse.

LIFE LESSONS:

Don't throw the Bypass Trust in the trash too quickly. For larger estates, the Bypass Trust might be better than the All to Spouse Plan with Optional Disclaimer Trust. While the Bypass Trust allows the surviving spouse to decide who gets what after the surviving spouse dies, the surviving spouse cannot tweak the final distribution of the Disclaimer Trust assets. The drug-addicted child, for example, will get the remaining assets. Further, the Bypass Trust doesn't require the surviving spouse to jump through all the Qualified Disclaimer hoops (e.g., exercising the option to disclaim within nine months), which the surviving spouse could easily mess up. Revisiting your goals (see Step # 2) will help you make the right decision. If your primary goals are simplicity and flexibility rather than protecting the assets from the IRS, Sexy Sue or Don Juan, you might prefer the All to Spouse Plan with Optional Disclaimer Trust. Carefully assess the pros and cons before making a final decision.

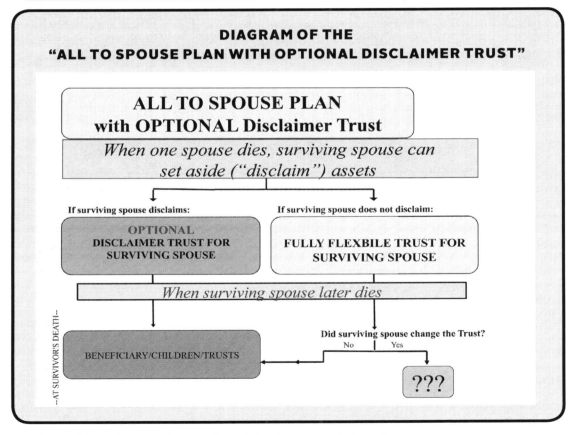

Abracadabra: Bypass Trust + Q-tip Election = a Third Option

While traditionally we either created a Living Trust with the Bypass Trust or the All to Spouse Plan with Optional Disclaimer for a married couple, after passage of the Taxpayer Relief Act we now consider a third option—a Bypass Trust that can be converted into an Irrevocable Trust after one spouse dies, referred to in this book as a "QTIP-Protection Trust." Basically, after the conversion, the Bypass Trust becomes what legal experts call a QTIP Trust, an Irrevocable Trust that protects the assets without the adverse income tax consequences of a Bypass Trust.

Basically, this type of trust is a Bypass Trust drafted to allow the surviving spouse to make a simple tax election (which your tax advisor will call a "Q-tip Election") that will eliminate the income tax bill that might be created with the Bypass Trust. Some experts refer to this type of Bypass Trust as a QTIPable Bypass Trust. If the surviving spouse makes a timely Q-tip Election (within 15 months after the first spouse's death assuming an Application for Extension of Time to File a Return is filed), the election in effect converts the Bypass Trust to a QTIP-Protection Trust. As the name implies, the QTIP-Protection Trust protects the trust assets from creditors, from Sexy Sue and Don Juan, and from potential capital gains on the sale of appreciated assets after the surviving spouse dies.

The QTIP-Protection Trust allows the surviving spouse to decide after the first death whether estate tax protection is necessary. If so, the survivor will keep the assets in the Bypass Trust. If not, the surviving spouse would make the Q-tip Election.

The QTIP-Protection Trust is perfect for the couple who may need estate tax protection, but who also want the protection against creditors or a future spouse. What if the surviving spouse falls in love with Sexy Sue or a charming Don Juan and is lured into relinquishing all the assets? What if creditors, like someone who falls in your home or a disgruntled employee, attack the assets, leaving nothing for the children or other ultimate beneficiaries?

The QTIP-Protection Trust can prevent the trust assets from going to Sexy Sue and Don Juan without the adverse income tax consequence of a Bypass Trust. Simple drafting of the Living Trust is designed to allow the surviving spouse to file a tax return making a "Q-tip Election." Abracadabra—the Bypass Trust will become an Irrevocable Trust with all the protection of the traditional Bypass Trust.

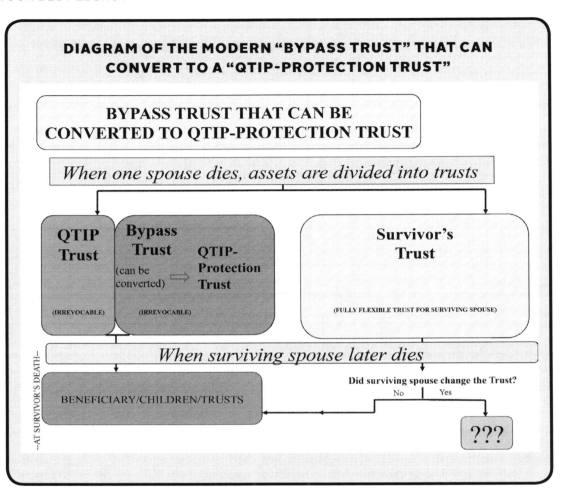

DIAGRAM OF THE MODERN "BYPASS TRUST" THAT CAN CONVERT TO A "QTIP-PROTECTION TRUST"

BYPASS TRUST THAT CAN BE CONVERTED TO QTIP-PROTECTION TRUST

When one spouse dies, assets are divided into trusts

QTIP Trust
(IRREVOCABLE)

Bypass Trust
(can be converted) ⇒ **QTIP-Protection Trust**
(IRREVOCABLE)

Survivor's Trust
(FULLY FLEXIBLE TRUST FOR SURVIVING SPOUSE)

When surviving spouse later dies

—AT SURVIVOR'S DEATH—

BENEFICIARY/CHILDREN/TRUSTS

Did surviving spouse change the Trust?
No   Yes

???

Caveat: Talk to your tax advisor about the ability to make a QTIP Election at the death of one spouse when the election is not needed to minimize estate tax. As this book is going to print, we are waiting for clarification from the IRS about this issue, which will impact the ability to convert a Bypass Trust to a QTIP Trust-Protection Trust. Also, talk to your attorney and tax advisor about back-up provisions in the trust to minimize the potential adverse tax consequence of the traditional Bypass Trust, such as giving an Independent Trustee the power to amend and giving the Trustee the power to distribute assets from a Bypass Trust outright to the surviving spouse.

One Size Fits All? No—the Size of the Estate Often Dictates the Type of Living Trust
Estates, like people, come in all shapes and sizes. You need to know your size before you shop for clothing, and you need to know the size of your estate before you determine what kind of estate plan you need. In the estate planning store, a small estate has less than $5 million of assets, a medium estate between $5 million and $10 million of assets, and a large estate over $10 million of assets. Your needs will vary depending on whether you are a "Small Estate Couple," "Medium Estate Couple" or "Large Estate Couple."

Be careful about categorizing yourself as a "Medium Estate Couple" or "Large Estate Couple." A seemingly medium or large estate with lots of retirement accounts that pass <u>outside</u> of a Living Trust might be more accurately categorized as a "Small Estate" or "Medium Estate" for determining the right type of Living Trust. First, calculate the current value of all non-retirement assets. Then, add all life insurance that will be paid to the Living Trust because you will be naming the Living Trust as the beneficiary on the Beneficiary Designation form provided by your insurance agent. Once you have the total, you will know if, for purposes of this section of the book, you have a small, medium or large estate.

Important: Your estate plan should be designed in case you die or become incapacitated within the next three years. Therefore, in determining the type of Living Trust you prefer, look at your current assets and net worth. However, if your estate might grow to become subject to estate tax, consider the anticipated future growth of your assets by implementing additional planning to minimize estate tax.

~ Size Small Couples: Assets Under $5 Million~

Couples with assets under $5 million need to focus on avoiding the time and expense of probate court, and likely don't need complicated trusts to minimize estate tax. Their assets are less than what one Exemption shelters from estate tax.

SIZE SMALL COUPLES: THROW THE TRADITIONAL BYPASS TRUST IN THE TRASH

Small estate couples should rarely create a Living Trust that requires assets to fund a traditional Bypass Trust after the death of the first spouse. All appreciated assets in the Bypass Trust will be subject to income tax when sold after the surviving spouse dies. While the Bypass Trust will not save estate tax, because the couple's assets are below the amount that can transfer without estate tax, it may result in capital gains tax that could have been avoided if the assets had not been transferred into the Bypass Trust.

SIZE SMALL COUPLES: BENEFITS OF THE BYPASS TRUST CONVERTIBLE TO A QTIP-PROTECTION TRUST

Although size small couples typically would never have a traditional Bypass Trust (they don't need it to reduce estate tax unless the law changes and the Exemption is lowered), they should consider a Bypass Trust that can be converted into a QTIP-Protection Trust. If one of your goals in Step #2 is to protect the assets from Sexy Sue or Don Juan or to protect the assets from creditors, the QTIP-Protection Trust will serve that goal without the adverse income tax consequence of the traditional

Bypass Trust. The QTIP-Protection Trust protects the assets, but because the assets should get a step up in the income tax basis when the surviving spouse dies, the sale of appreciated assets at that time should not trigger income tax.

SIZE SMALL COUPLES: BENEFITS OF THE ALL TO SPOUSE PLAN WITH OPTIONAL DISCLAIMER TRUST

Small estate couples not concerned about assets going to a new spouse and not worried about creditors will appreciate the simplicity of the All to Spouse Plan with Optional Disclaimer Trust. Couples who have been married for a long time, have children from their marriage (and none from previous marriages), and have no concerns about giving the surviving spouse full and absolute power over the trust assets will simplify life for the surviving settlor by not having her hassle with the administration of an ongoing Irrevocable Trust that she may not need. Unless the surviving spouse disclaims assets, she won't have to file annual tax returns for the trust or account to remainder beneficiaries, who may be sitting in wait to inherit what remains.

The All to Spouse Plan protects the assets from estate tax, but only if such protection is needed (either because the Exemption decreased or because the assets increased). If needed, the surviving spouse would simply "disclaim" assets, and the Trustee would fund those assets into a Disclaimer Trust. However, because the asset value is already small enough to avoid estate tax, the surviving spouse would probably not disclaim and so she would not have the administration hassle of the Irrevocable Disclaimer Trust. Assuming she doesn't disclaim, the surviving spouse has unbridled discretion to use all the assets and decide who gets them when she dies.

SIZE SMALL COUPLES: DOWNSIDE OF THE ALL TO SPOUSE PLAN WITH OPTIONAL DISCLAIMER

Unfortunately, the All to Spouse Plan with Optional Disclaimer Trust offers zero protection for the surviving spouse (or for the remainder beneficiaries, likely the kids!). If the deceased spouse has large debts or gets sued and loses, the creditors can seize her assets. Or, if the survivor re-marries and leaves all the assets to her new love, the children or other intended beneficiaries will get nothing. While the All to Spouse Plan offers the surviving spouse simplicity and ease of administration, unless the surviving spouse disclaims, the spouse who dies first has no idea where his assets will end up.

The Bottom Line: Size small couples who aren't worried about possible lawsuits or a second spouse should strongly consider the All to Spouse Plan with Optional Disclaimer Trust. Those who are worried about lawsuits, Sexy Sue or Don Juan should instead choose the QTIP-Protection Trust, which is basically a Bypass Trust with special provisions designed to protect the assets without the adverse income tax consequences of the traditional Bypass Trust.

~ Medium Estate Couples: Assets Between $5 Million and $10 Million ~

Couples with assets between $5 million and $10 million need to focus on minimizing estate tax. Because their assets exceed what one Exemption can shelter from estate tax, they likely need a plan to minimize estate tax when the surviving spouse dies.

Size medium couples have a critical decision to make if they don't want their heirs or other intended beneficiaries to pay estate tax. Typically, they would either use a Living Trust with an Irrevocable Trust like the traditional Bypass Trust or take advantage of so-called "portability" under the Taxpayer Relief Act, which enables couples to use the Exemption of both spouses. Both have pros and cons: the Bypass Trust lacks flexibility and can result in income tax on the sale of appreciated assets after the surviving spouse dies, but, as you will read below, relying only on portability may prove disastrous. Medium estate couples will want to consider a third option.

Some people think that the Taxpayer Relief Act makes estate planning simpler. But, in reality, it necessitates more creative analysis so that the size medium couple doesn't cause a burden to their friends or family in higher income tax or unexpected estate tax.

SIZE MEDIUM COUPLES: BENEFITS OF THE BYPASS TRUST CONVERTIBLE TO A QTIP-PROTECTION TRUST

Without some planning—either forming a Bypass Trust or relying on the surviving spouse to file the necessary estate tax return to elect portability—the ultimate recipients of the size medium couple's assets will pay estate tax. However, locking into a traditional Bypass Trust could be a huge mistake for size medium couples.

The traditional Bypass Trust may not be needed if the surviving spouse files the necessary tax return to elect to "port" or transfer the deceased spouse's Exemption to the surviving spouse, and may even prove disastrous. In other words, the Bypass Trust may not save a dime in estate tax but may result in increased *income tax* if appreciated assets are sold.

Therefore, when using an Irrevocable Trust to minimize estate tax at the surviving spouse's death or to protect the assets from creditors, Sexy Sue or Don Juan, size medium couples should consider provisions in the Bypass Trust so that it can be converted into a QTIP-Protection Trust. This type of trust is like permanent insurance—the assets funded into a properly drafted and administered Bypass Trust, including all appreciation, will avoid estate tax no matter whether the surviving spouse files an estate tax return or re-marries.

The Bypass Trust that can be converted to a QTIP-Protection Trust is flexible. The surviving spouse can wait until after the first spouse dies to evaluate whether the estate will be subject to estate tax. If so, the surviving spouse can consider keeping some assets in the traditional Bypass Trust (and she may also file an estate tax return to port her deceased spouse's unused Exemption). If not, assuming the IRS allows the tax election, she can convert the Bypass Trust to a QTIP-Protection Trust by making a Q-tip Election for some of the deceased spouse's assets.

The Bypass Trust that can be converted to a QTIP-Protection Trust (1) locks in who gets the deceased spouse's assets after the surviving spouse dies (sorry Sexy Sue, you are out of luck!), and (2) avoids adverse income tax consequences of a traditional Bypass Trust when the Bypass Trust is not needed to minimize estate tax (i.e., it avoids the double whammy of no estate tax savings at the surviving spouse's death, but increased income tax upon the sale of appreciated assets).

The Bypass Trust that can be converted into a QTIP-Protection Trust also offers the surviving spouse important discretion to direct where the assets go when the survivor dies. Although Sexy Sue and Don Juan are out of luck, the couple can give the surviving spouse some latitude to make changes. If the surviving spouse has a falling out with those named in the Living Trust, for example, the convertible Bypass Trust could give the surviving spouse discretion to adjust the final distribution of the trust assets, which in legalese is called a "Power of Appointment." The Bypass Trust, even if converted into a QTIP-Protection Trust, can give the surviving spouse the power to appoint the assets to a group of people (i.e., the kids), but without the unbridled discretion to leave the assets to Sexy Sue or Don Juan.

SIZE MEDIUM COUPLES: BENEFITS OF THE ALL TO SPOUSE PLAN WITH OPTIONAL DISCLAIMER TRUST

If the size medium couple don't care about protecting assets, either because they don't have rental property or a business that puts them at higher risk for being sued, they don't worry about lawsuits, or they don't think their spouse would ever give their assets to a Sexy Sue or Don Juan (because they have been married a gazillion years), the All to Spouse Plan and Optional Disclaimer Trust can be beneficial. The surviving spouse won't automatically be locked into administering an Irrevocable Trust (like a Bypass Trust or QTIP-Protection Trust). Instead, the surviving spouse will have nine months after a spouse dies to make that decision. Waiting until after the death of the first spouse will enable the surviving spouse to make a better decision compared to a Living Trust with a Bypass Trust, where the decision is made years before.

Under the All to Spouse Plan, the surviving spouse can wait and see what's needed *after* one spouse dies. Then, the survivor can decide whether to disclaim assets, in which case the Trustee will fund the Irrevocable Trust called a Disclaimer Trust and/or file an estate tax return electing to port (meaning transfer) the unused Exemption of the first spouse to minimize estate tax when the surviving spouse dies.

SIZE MEDIUM COUPLES: DOWNSIDE OF THE ALL TO SPOUSE PLAN

If size medium couple Harold and Barbara created an All to Spouse Plan, and Harold was so distraught after Barbara's death that he did nothing for two years, he blew it. Where the Bypass Trust plan creates insurance within the estate tax planning, the All to Spouse Plan has none. Once Harold misses the deadline to "disclaim" assets or to file an estate tax return electing "portability," his beneficiaries are out of luck—their loss, the IRS's gain.

With the All to Spouse Plan, a couple that turns out to require estate tax protection could inadvertently mess up the optional Disclaimer, which might be very costly for the beneficiaries, who would pay the estate tax that could have been avoided had the surviving spouse acted timely. Even something simple like listing the assets on a loan application before the disclaimer could cause adverse tax consequences.

A Living Trust with a Bypass Trust that can later be converted to a QTIP-Protection Trust doesn't have the same strict deadlines as the All to Spouse Plan with Optional Disclaimer Trust; the Q-tip Election needs to be done within 15 months rather than

the 9-month deadline of a disclaimer, and even if the surviving spouse doesn't make the Q-tip Election, she has the safety net of a traditional Bypass Trust that could save estate tax. If a distraught or emotional surviving spouse might neglect the necessary post-death estate planning required in an All to Spouse Plan, that size medium couple will want a Bypass Trust that can convert into a QTIP-Protection Trust.

The Bottom Line: Size medium couples concerned about possible lawsuits or a second spouse will almost always choose a Bypass Trust that can be converted to a QTIP-Protection Trust and will include other trust provisions, like Independent Trustee powers to amend the trust and Trustee powers to withdraw assets from the trust in case the QTIP Election fails. These couples won't want to be stuck with the traditional Bypass Trust that might leave them with an income tax bill on appreciated assets without any estate tax savings. If they forgo the Bypass Trust completely and create an All to Spouse Plan with Optional Disclaimer Trust, their assets might appreciate so much that the survivor's estate might exceed the Exemption allowed—even if the surviving spouse elects to port the unused Exemption of the first spouse. Or, the surviving spouse may inadvertently fail to take the necessary steps after a death to minimize estate tax. Locking the survivor into an ongoing Irrevocable Trust, like a Bypass Trust that can be converted to a QTIP-Protection Trust, safeguards the assets.

Therefore, although some size medium couples who have been married a long time and share children (but no stepchildren) may prefer the All to Spouse Plan with Disclaimer Trust Option for its flexibility, they should first explore the Bypass Trust that the surviving spouse can convert to a QTIP-Protection Trust.

The convertible Bypass Trust provides the surviving spouse time to determine whether the size of the estate warrants keeping the estate tax protection of the Bypass Trust, or whether to file an estate tax return and make a Q-tip election to convert the Bypass Trust to a QTIP-Protection Trust. If the Q-tip Election is made, the assets remain in a protected Irrevocable Trust (the QTIP-Protection Trust) for the lifetime use of the surviving spouse, but without the adverse income tax consequences of a traditional Bypass Trust.

By creating a Living Trust with special provisions that allow the Bypass Trust to convert into a QTIP-Protection Trust, couples can have their cake and eat it too; the surviving spouse doesn't have to worry about adhering to the strict and unforgiving administrative steps needed to disclaim assets as required by the All to

Spouse Plan with Optional Disclaimer Trust, but, if needed, an Irrevocable Trust will be funded that saves estate tax, if needed, and if not needed is converted into a QTIP-Protection Trust that can safeguard the assets from creditors in case of a lawsuit or from Sexy Sue or Don Juan in case of re-marriage.

LIFE LESSONS:

One of the biggest mistakes couples make is keeping life insurance out of a trust. Couples with life insurance should either create an Irrevocable Trust during their lifetime to hold their insurance or name their Living Trust as the beneficiary of their insurance. Naming the Living Trust allows the insurance proceeds at death to fund whatever Irrevocable Trusts are included in the Living Trust, such as the (convertible) Bypass Trust or Disclaimer Trust, which protects the proceeds and could minimize estate tax when the surviving spouse dies.

~ Large Estate Couples: Assets over $10 million ~

Couples with more than $10 million in assets must focus on minimizing estate tax because their assets exceed both of their Exemptions. Therefore, most size large couples need a traditional Bypass Trust (plus other planning techniques like life-time gifting or the selling of assets, which can and should be further explored with a tax advisor).

SIZE LARGE COUPLES: BENEFITS OF
THE TRADITIONAL BYPASS TRUST

There are at least five major benefits of the traditional Bypass Trust for many size large couples:

1. Under a Bypass Trust, the assets *plus appreciation* pass transfer tax-free.
2. The Bypass Trust has the smallest possible margin for inadvertent post-death mistakes. Even if the surviving spouse fails to consult an attorney after the first spouse dies, the Bypass Trust can be "late funded"[3] and still pass transfer-tax free.
3. The Bypass Trust assets can pass to children and then to grandchildren free of transfer tax, which cannot be accomplished using portability[4] when the estate exceeds the value that one Exemption can shelter.

4. A Bypass Trust protects the assets from being left to a second spouse instead of to children or other individuals chosen by the deceased spouse.

5. A Bypass Trust can be drafted to protect assets in case of a lawsuit so that creditors don't take assets that should go to your family and loved ones.

LIFE LESSONS:

Size large couples should consider additional advanced planning to minimize their estate tax. Here are a few basic examples:

❖ *Buying living insurance in the name of an Irrevocable Trust could be a life-line for family members, while also avoiding estate tax on the life insurance proceeds.*

❖ *Lifetime gifts of interest in a business can reduce estate tax and provide the necessary framework for the continuity of a family business.*

❖ *Annual gifting within the so-called "Annual Exclusion" can reduce estate tax, without any filing requirements.*

❖ *Gifts to Irrevocable Trusts for beneficiaries can enable assets to grow for future generations.*

The optimal time to plan a large estate is before asset values get close to the Exemption. Don't be the 80-year-old asking, "How do I minimize estate tax?" Don't let your children ask this same question when they realize their inheritance is going to the IRS. By then, it's too late!

Critical Fact #4: Portability Is a New and Powerful Method to Minimize Estate Tax If Used Effectively

The ability to port the Exemption from a deceased spouse to a surviving spouse could eliminate estate tax after the death of both spouses, without the need for complicated trusts! By filing a simplified estate tax return after one spouse dies, the surviving spouse can elect to port or transfer the unused Exemption of her deceased spouse.

In effect, by making the simple portability election on an estate tax return, a surviving spouse can now use the available Exemption of both spouses. While a couple could always potentially use the Exemption of two people, now one spouse can use the double exemption even after one spouse dies without creating any ongoing Irrevocable Trusts. In 2014, when a U.S citizen or resident can transfer $5.34 million free of transfer tax, a couple could transfer double that—a total of $10.68 million—after one spouse dies, just by electing portability on a timely filed estate tax return.

After one spouse dies, if the surviving spouse might have more assets than her own Exemption can shelter from transfer tax, she will want to understand the benefit of being able to use her spouse's available Exemption in addition to her own Exemption. A surviving spouse who may have a taxable estate when she dies would consider electing portability if:

- ❖ One spouse dies before the couple created an estate plan.
- ❖ The Bypass Trust is funded with less than the full amount of the deceased spouse's Exemption.
- ❖ The first spouse to die has retirement accounts that pass outside of the Living Trust.
- ❖ The surviving spouse did not disclaim assets, either intentionally or inadvertently.

In a blended family with children from a prior marriage, consider adding instructions in the Will requiring the Executor to file an estate tax return electing portability. Otherwise, for example, a stepson appointed as the Executor of his dad's Will might not want to spend the trust's money to file a tax return electing portability if the election will benefit his stepmother's kids, not himself. A simple instruction in the Will that the Executor must file an estate tax return to elect portability whenever doing so will minimize estate tax after the second death will avoid conflicts after a spouse dies.

In each of the situations above, by electing portability, the unused Exemption of the deceased spouse can be added to the surviving spouse's Exemption, which could save estate tax at the surviving spouse's death. Accordingly, the surviving spouse will file an estate tax return electing portability if the surviving spouse's estate may exceed her Exemption and therefore be subject to estate tax.

Electing portability can be especially important to hedge against the possibility that the Exemption in effect at the surviving spouse's death might be lowered. Even if the surviving spouse's assets are much less than the Exemption when the first spouse dies, if a new law lowers the Exemption in effect when the surviving spouse dies, electing portability could ensure that the kids won't pay estate tax even if the Exemption is lower.

Generally, no estate tax is due when one spouse dies, and before the Taxpayer Relief Act, a surviving spouse with a small estate would never file a tax return at the first death. However, because portability requires an election on a timely estate tax return, after the Taxpayer Relief Act more surviving spouses will be filing an estate tax return to elect portability.

> *Don't Neglect to Elect:* When Sally's husband died, she assumed she didn't need to file an estate tax return because no estate tax was due. This assumption was false. If her estate is worth more than the Exemption *when she dies*, then her failure to file a tax return to elect portability may cost her children tens of thousands of dollars in estate tax due after her death.

CREATIVE PLANNING CAN EXPONENTIALLY INCREASE THE BENEFITS OF ELECTING PORTABILITY

While portability can minimize estate tax for many couples, additional planning can exponentially increase the value of the portability election for couples with large estates. Once the surviving spouse elects portability, she could further minimize her estate tax by gifting during her lifetime, which helps for many reasons.

First, lifetime gifts ensure that the surviving spouse won't lose the benefit of the ported Exemption because of remarriage and death of a new spouse. Once she gifts the assets and uses the ported Exemption, she immediately reaps the benefits by reducing her taxable estate.

Second, lifetime gifts can leverage the Exemption, meaning that for every dollar of Exemption used by a gift, she can move more than a dollar out of her taxable estate. The surviving spouse, for example, might use $1 million of her Exemption to gift $1.4 million of assets by transferring a small interest in a business or in real estate and obtaining an appraisal that substantiates a 40% discounted value of the gifted assets. Further, when she dies, the value of the fractional interest in her asset that remains in her estate might also be discounted for purposes of calculating the estate tax due upon her demise. Using part of her Exemption to give only five percent of an asset, for example, could save a bundle in estate tax if the IRS accepts a discounted value of the assets that remain in the surviving spouse's estate. While portability is good news, it gets even better when implemented with other gifting strategies.

IT'S NOT AN "EITHER OR" GAME: BEWARE OF RELYING EXCLUSIVELY ON PORTABILITY OR ON THE BYPASS TRUST TO MINIMIZE TAX

Some couples mistakenly think that their estate plan will either rely exclusively on electing portability or on funding ongoing Irrevocable Trusts, such as a traditional Bypass Trust. In fact, it's often not an "either or" proposition; funding a Bypass Trust and electing portability are not mutually exclusive.

A surviving spouse may need to fund a Bypass Trust *and* elect portability. For example, if the estate includes retirement accounts, only the non-retirement assets will typically fund the Bypass Trust. Therefore, the Bypass Trust may not use up all of the deceased spouse's Exemption. A $1 million IRA, for example, which passes directly to the surviving spouse and not to the Bypass Trust will require a portability election to shelter the IRA from estate tax when the survivor dies if the surviving spouse doesn't have enough of her own Exemption to shelter it.

Similarly, relying only on a portability election could cause big problems. While the ability of one spouse to port the unused Exemption of the deceased spouse can minimize estate tax at the second death, many couples with large estates need additional estate planning because portability has serious pitfalls:

❖ The amount of Exemption ported to the survivor is fixed upon the deceased spouse's death at a certain dollar amount, without any annual increases. Therefore, although the survivor's assets may be invested and grow, the Exemption to shelter those assets from estate tax when the survivor dies will not grow. Accordingly, unlike the Bypass Trust protection of the appreciation on the Bypass Trust assets, the ported Exemption may not be enough to shelter the appreciation of the assets.

❖ If the surviving spouse remarries and the second spouse dies, the surviving spouse loses the first spouse's unused Exemption and instead gets the unused Exemption of the second spouse, which might be much lower than the unused Exemption of the first spouse. In other words, the ported Exemption is not guaranteed—it can be lost in the event of re-marriage if the new spouse dies.

❖ Portability cannot shelter transfer tax on certain transfers to grandchildren, and the "use it or lose it rule" still applies. Accordingly, if a grandparent wants to pass assets to a grandchild and allocate the Exemption so that it passes free of transfer tax, the Exemption must be allocated at that grandparent's death. Any unused Exemption of the additional tax on generation skipping transfers that would otherwise

apply cannot be ported or transferred to a surviving grandparent. Therefore, for couples with large estates wanting to keep assets in multigenerational trusts, the ABC Living Trust will continue to be the planning strategy of choice.

The Bottom Line: Because portability has pitfalls, it can and often should be used in conjunction with other planning to minimize estate tax, rather than alone as the sole plan for minimizing estate tax. Further, simply because a Living Trust instructs for assets to be funded into a traditional Bypass Trust doesn't mean that an estate tax return should not be filed electing portability.

Although the post Taxpayer Relief Act era simplified plans for some couples, assessing when to rely on portability, when to include a traditional Bypass Trust and when to do both exemplifies the complexity of this new era of estate planning.

> **LIFE LESSON:**
>
> *Don't assume that, because no estate tax is due, no estate tax return needs to be filed. The only way to elect portability is on a timely filed estate tax return.*

Critical Fact #5: Assets Must Be Transferred into the Living Trust

Dave called me a few years ago, irate. His mother had just died. She had a Living Trust that left everything to him, but he had just learned that his mother also had a separate $1,000,000 bank account. The money in that account had all passed to his brother instead of him. Dave was baffled about how that could have happened.

The answer was simple. Dave's mother prepared a Living Trust, but never transferred the bank account into the Living Trust. The account that went to Dave's brother was titled with his brother's name and his mother as "Joint Tenants." Whenever people own an asset as a "Joint Tenants" and one named person dies, the asset goes to the other named person. When Dave's mother died, her bank account that was titled as Joint Tenants went directly to the other named Joint Tenant, Dave's brother. Her Living Trust was irrelevant in determining who got the bank account.

The bank never requested a copy of the Living Trust or the Will, nor did it need to. The title of the account alone required the bank to transfer it directly to Dave's brother, regardless of the Living Trust that left everything to Dave. Had his mother changed the title of the account to the Living Trust, Dave would have received the $1,000,000 bank account, but he didn't because his mother probably didn't know that she needed to change title on the account to the Living Trust.

Robert's mother also had a Living Trust and never transferred all her assets into the trust. Unlike Dave's mother, Robert's mother listed the home on the schedule of assets at the end of the Living Trust, and she did not hold title to the home as Joint Tenants. Because the home wasn't in the trust, when Robert's mother died, Robert needed to file papers in court and obtain a signed Order from the judge stating that the home was included in the Living Trust. He then had to record the court Order before he could transfer the home by deed from his mother's trust to himself. Had Robert's mother transferred her home into the trust, none of this would have been needed.

Luckily however, because she listed the home on the schedule of assets attached to her Living Trust and held title in her own name, not as Joint Tenants, Robert was able to solve the problem with a court Order. Robert was more fortunate than Dave because at least he got his mom's home, but he had to spend thousands of dollars and jump over hurdles that easily could have been avoided.

Failing to transfer assets into your Living Trust can cost your intended beneficiaries thousands of dollars and months of administrative work to transfer the title of assets. It's almost always simpler and less expensive to transfer assets before death. At a minimum, every asset intended to be in the trust should be listed on the schedule at the end of the Living Trust. Although listing assets on the trust schedule does not transfer them to the Living Trust, the schedule does typically allow beneficiaries to file a petition for a court Order to get the assets into the Living Trust.

See the Appendix for sample instructions on transferring assets into a Living Trust. Talk to your advisor about properly transferring your assets.

Critical Fact #6: Different Types of Trusts Can Protect Your Children in Different Ways

IMPORTANT CONSIDERATIONS TO PROTECT YOUNGER CHILDREN
Only an 18-year-old thinks that 18 is the perfect age to inherit a lot of assets with no strings attached. Most parents want their children to be mature adults before relinquishing control over assets. They don't want an inheritance to spoil their children, they don't want assets left to their children's spouses in the case of divorce and they certainly don't want creditors to get their children's money.

As the rich get richer, more children will inherit more wealth and run the risk of becoming spoiled. Proper planning can ensure that an inheritance won't spoil children.

Certain estate planning and types of trusts help protect assets for children. But don't hold the purse strings too tight: Children can be devastated by stringent benchmarks that must be met to access inherited assets. For example, requiring that children earn a business degree before acquiring their inheritance—a true story—can torment a child whose passion is music or art. Despite cajoling our son to study medicine or law (every good child becomes a doctor or lawyer, right?), our oldest son majored in music in college. Now, we couldn't be happier that he followed his passion: He's a *working* musician, and he's doing what he loves. Kids should follow their passion. Estate plans that try to direct the careers of children are akin to parents trying to rule their children's lives from the grave. Such plans are generally ill-advised.

Similarly, requiring a college degree as a prerequisite to distribution can create an insurmountable obstacle to a child permanently disabled from a terrible car accident. Or, using the birth of a grandchild as a distribution benchmark inadvertently punishes the infertile child who chooses not to adopt. Rather than establishing benchmarks, you can ensure that good values are passed on to your children by setting broad guidelines in the trust statement and by putting the right person in charge as the Trustee—someone whose values you trust and admire.

The right kind of estate plan for children provides the right kind of protection; rather than giving assets to kids in their own individual name, consider creating an ongoing trust that will hold title to the assets. The trust becomes not only an instruction manual for how you want that money used, but also armor that helps protect the money.

Recently, I was celebrating my birthday with a long-time friend, and he shared how his parents' estate plan helped him defend a lawsuit. His parents, who died five years before the lawsuit, left their assets to him in an ongoing lifetime trust. When my friend's long-time business partner filed a lawsuit against him, the partner soon discovered that my friend had no assets in his name. The partner would not have been able to recover anything, even if he won the lawsuit, so the case was quickly settled. His parents were smart. Rather than leaving him their assets in his own name, they created an ongoing Irrevocable Trust that acts like a corporation, in that it's separate and apart from the individual that benefits from it. My friend was grateful for his parents' wisdom.

Unfortunately, not enough parents know how to protect their children properly. Either the plan spoils the kids, or it doesn't have adequate safeguards, meaning a son-in-law, daughter-in-law, or creditor can obtain the assets.

Under the law, children are adults at 18. Unless you make other provisions, your kids are legally entitled to inherit money at that young age. How many children who inherit a fortune at 18 are going to be committed enough to succeed in school, excel at their career, work hard, and become a good citizen who gives back to the community?

CHOOSE THE RIGHT TYPE OF IRREVOCABLE TRUST FOR YOUR CHILDREN

Often an ongoing Irrevocable Trust becomes the lifeline that will sustain and protect children. The Trustee in charge of the money while the kids are young can distribute money to them as needed for their support and education. Irrevocable Trusts for children come in different forms, such as **Sprinkling Trusts, Separate Share Trusts** and **Dynasty Trusts**.

The **Sprinkling Trust** allows the Trustee to distribute money to several children from one common bank account, without keeping track of who receives what. Just as a parent would, the Trustee can use the available trust funds to take care of the children. A Sprinkling Trust ensures that the kids' needs are met, without concern that each child receives an equal share.

When children are far apart in age, or when the children are older and each is to receive an equal portion of the assets, a so-called **Separate Share Trust** keeps the children's accounts separate, with expenses for each child coming from that child's separate bank account. The Separate Share Trust ensures that each child is treated equally, receiving an equal share of the trust assets.

While a Sprinkling Trust or Separate Share Trust protects an inheritance until the children are mature, perhaps at age 25 or 30, a **Dynasty Trust** lasts the whole lifetime of the children, adding even more protection. You can put the children in charge of their money as the Trustee when they are mature, rather than giving the assets to the children in their own name, individually. Keeping assets in a lifetime trust offers better protection than a trust that goes to the children individually at certain set ages.

The lifetime Dynasty Trust can be customized for your individual concerns. Because you won't be around to evaluate your children's ability to serve as the Trustee of their trust, you can appoint someone—either a family member or a trusted advisor—to determine when children are ready to be put in charge as the Trustee of their own trust. Or, you can appoint someone independent to act as Trustee, giving the children the right to hire and fire the Trustee, which could make it even harder for creditors to reach the assets than if the children act as their own Trustee. Trusts with so-called "fully discretionary" distribution provisions naming someone independent as the Trustee are considered to be better asset protection than trusts with the children in charge of all distribution decisions.

The ongoing lifetime Dynasty Trust can also be customized to ensure that the assets are preserved and distributed to grandchildren. If you leave assets directly to a child and then the child gets divorced, you may have just given <u>your assets</u> to your child's soon to be ex-spouse. If a child dies, you may be giving <u>your assets</u> to your child's spouse rather than your grandchildren. If the child's spouse then remarries, <u>your assets</u> may end up going to that new spouse, and not to your grandchildren. A Dynasty Trust can be drafted to address these issues.

All trusts for children, whether a Sprinkling Trust, Separate Share Trust or Dynasty Trust, can help avoid spoiling children and can add protection. Further, by including in the estate plan guidelines such as these for the Trustee to consider in distributing money from children's trusts, you can impact your children's lives forever:

- ❖ We intend to provide a continuing fund to assist in the health, education, support, and maintenance of our children and grandchildren.
- ❖ We hope that all our children will become self-supporting without having to rely on any sums provided to them under their respective trusts.
- ❖ We encourage our children to actively pursue their own chosen career goals by continuing any educational programs necessary to achieve such goals.
- ❖ We hope that our children will achieve success not only in an economic sense, but in all other aspects of the beneficiary's life necessary for personal happiness so that our children achieve success on their own merits, without having to rely on the sums distributed from the trust.
- ❖ We want the Trustee to consider whether the distribution will assist, but not supplant, the children's' educational goals, charitable goals, and work ethic and whether the children are leading a life free of substance and alcohol abuse.

The right trust for your children can protect them and their assets and help them develop into upstanding citizens. By sharing your goals and dreams for your children, you can create a lasting legacy for generations to come.

LIFE LESSONS:

While Dynasty Trusts have many benefits, and we encourage larger net worth clients to consider them, be aware of the downside: A Dynasty Trust is more complicated to administer during the lifetime of the children, more expensive for an attorney to draft than a trust that will terminate when the child reaches a certain age, requires ongoing separate income tax returns for the lifetime of your children and, without proper drafting, can increase income tax that could otherwise be avoided. Therefore, seek legal advice before deciding to create a Dynasty Trust for your children, and never draft a Dynasty Trust yourself. Engage an attorney trained and experienced in this type of planning.

Critical Fact #7: An Irrevocable Trust Funded During Life Can Play a Critical Role in Your Estate Plan

BENEFITS OF FUNDING IRREVOCABLE TRUSTS DURING LIFETIME

In addition to creating the more common Living Trust, those who have significant wealth, meaning their assets exceed the Exemption that can be left free of estate tax, can and should explore the benefits of transferring assets to Irrevocable Trusts while they are living. Irrevocable Trusts, typically designed to reduce estate tax at death when created and funded during the drafter's lifetime, offer wide-ranging benefits.

Anyone with assets more than the Exemption who doesn't need the assets for support should evaluate whether to gift or sell assets to Irrevocable Trusts during lifetime. A lifetime transfer, especially of a fractional interest (e.g., giving or selling 50%, or some other partial interest, of rental property to the Irrevocable Trust) or of a future interest (e.g., transferring a primary residence to an Irrevocable Trust, but keeping the right to live in it for the next 10 years), typically passes more wealth and saves more estate tax than any Irrevocable Trust funded at death.

Properly drafted Irrevocable Trusts can be extremely flexible. You can name an Independent Trustee with the power to change the terms of an Irrevocable Trust. Further, even if you cannot act as Trustee for tax reasons, you can often retain the right to fire the Trustee and appoint a new one; while technically you relinquish control over the assets in an Irrevocable Trust, you can in fact maintain a certain amount of control under a properly drafted and administered Irrevocable Trust. Further, in states such as Nevada, you may even be able to create a trust in which you can be added into the trust as a possible trust beneficiary should you need the gifted assets.

COMPARISON OF IRREVOCABLE TRUSTS AND LIVING TRUSTS

Irrevocable Trusts are quite different than Living Trusts.

—A funded Living Trust avoids probate; Irrevocable Trusts can allow asset transfer during one's lifetime (either by gifting the asset or selling it to the trust) so that, upon death, *the assets and all the growth and appreciation on those assets* are not subject to estate tax.

—A Living Trust can be amended or revoked during life; an Irrevocable Trust created during life cannot be amended or revoked without jumping through legal hoops.

—A Living Trust does not have a separate tax ID number while the creator is still living; an Irrevocable Trust created during life requires a separate tax ID number and often the annual filing of an income tax return.

—A Living Trust offers no protection from lawsuits or creditors during life; an Irrevocable Trust can protect assets for vulnerable beneficiaries like children and can protect assets from spendthrifts. Even life insurance can be purchased in an Irrevocable Trust, thereby exempting the insurance proceeds from estate tax and adding protection in the event of a lawsuit.

CHOOSE LIFE OVER DEATH

Married couples can create Living Trusts that provide for the funding of an Irrevocable Trust, like a Bypass Trust, at death. However, a couple whose assets will be subject to estate tax when the surviving spouse dies even with the shelter offered by the Bypass Trust should consider additional planning, such as selling or gifting assets to an Irrevocable Trust during their lifetime.

> *Wise Grandpa:* Grandpa Gary created an Irrevocable Trust for his young grandkids so that they wouldn't spend all the money he was giving them during his lifetime. If he gifted $1 million to the Irrevocable Trust and it doubled in value to $2 million, none of it would be subject to estate tax when Grandpa Gary dies. Using only $1 million of his Exemption, he in essence transferred $2 million out of his estate.

Creating ongoing Irrevocable Trusts before death can also protect other adult spendthrifts. One woman had the nicest brother, but he was totally incapable of handling his own finances. He got himself into huge debt and anytime he obtained any money he squandered it within weeks. The woman kept giving her brother money to bail him out, but her help was counterproductive.

The woman told her brother that she would only continue helping him if he agreed to put his assets into an Irrevocable Trust. It worked beautifully. The brother

transferred all his assets into an Irrevocable Trust, naming his sister as the Trustee. That way, the brother could no longer make irresponsible decisions with his money because he was no longer in charge. The Irrevocable Trust enabled the sister to keep helping her brother while maintaining control of her brother's finances for his own protection.

LIFE LESSONS (AND FOOD FOR THOUGHT WHEN YOU TALK TO YOUR TAX ADVISOR):

Gifting the so-called "Annual Exclusion" amount to an Irrevocable Trust and then having the Trustee buy life insurance can shelter all the life insurance from estate tax when you die while preserving all of your Exemption to shelter other assets. Even if you gift more than the Annual Exclusion, you can file a gift tax return and use some of the Exemption so that you don't have to pay any gift tax on the gift. Using the gift to buy insurance can leverage your Exemption. For example, if you use $500,000 of your Exemption by gifting that amount to the Irrevocable Trust, you can pass a lot more than the Exemption used estate tax free, because $500,000 will buy more than a $500,000 life insurance policy. Using only $500,000 of Exemption can pass millions of dollars in wealth in the form of life insurance.

If you create an Irrevocable Trust to hold life insurance, referred to as an ILIT, do not pay the insurance premiums directly. Instead, gift money annually to the ILIT, precisely following all the instructions about the required notices to the beneficiaries; let the Trustee write a check from the ILIT bank account to pay the insurance premiums. If you don't follow all the rules provided by your tax advisor, the IRS will tax the life insurance as if you had never held it in the Irrevocable Life Insurance Trust.

Critical Fact #8: For International Estate Planning Issues, Hire a Specialist

David, a single parent who is a French citizen living in California, inquires about a Living Trust. If he dies, he wants his eight-year-old daughter to live in France with his sister, who will supervise his money. David should seek the advice of an attorney who specializes in international issues.

If you answer "yes" to any of the following questions, then your estate plan is not complete without consulting an international estate-planning attorney:

1. Are you a non-U.S. citizen or resident for estate tax purposes? (Important: U.S. residency for estate tax purposes is not the same as U.S. residency for income tax purposes.)
2. Is your spouse a non-U.S. citizen?
3. Do you own property outside of the U.S.?
4. Do you intend to name a Trustee who is not a U.S. citizen or resident?
5. Do you plan to move outside of the U.S. at any time in the future?
6. Do you want your children to live with a guardian outside of the U.S.?

Talk to an estate planning attorney and get a referral to an international specialist if necessary. Ask the specialist about all international estate planning issues that might affect you.

Critical Fact #9: Take Three Precautions to Avoid Family Feuds

Family feuds are a real and devastating consequence of inadequate estate planning.

> *A Family Feud:* A homebound elderly man wanted to change his trust. An attorney came to his home, and they proceeded to meet several more times. About a year after the first meeting, the man signed a revised Living Trust without notifying any of his family that he had changed his plan.
>
> His revised Living Trust gave most of his assets to a charity, excluding his niece and other family members. He also removed his niece as the Trustee of the trust and appointed a friend instead.

When the niece learned about the revised plan, she called the County's Adult Protective Services. Petitions were filed in court to declare the elderly man incompetent and to invalidate the last trust. The niece even filed a lawsuit against the attorney who prepared the revised trust, claiming he should have known that her uncle lacked capacity to sign the revised plan. Before the man had even died, his family had spent three years and more than $100,000 of his money fighting in court to invalidate the plan he had created.

The niece would have been much less likely to sue had her uncle taken some of the precautions discussed below. Following three simple practices can often prevent family feuds.

1. *Obtain documentation of capacity and a waiver to challenge capacity*

Have a physician examine a person who is sick or elderly and document the testing and conclusions that prove the person has legal capacity to sign the estate plan. Otherwise, heirs may challenge the enforceability of the estate plan under a legal theory called "lack of capacity." When it's clear that the person has capacity, videotape the person at the signing meeting explaining, for example, what he owns, what he's signing, identifying his family and outlining who is to receive the assets under the document being signed. One elderly mother even obtained a written waiver from her three children, indicating that they would never challenge her capacity to sign her revised estate plan; when she died the assets were distributed without any fighting.

2. *Never plan in secrecy; obtain a waiver of the right to contest the plan*

A secret plan is almost always a bad plan, one that can result in fighting.

> *Shhh!:* One 94-year-old man living in a residential care facility called an attorney to revise his plan. Having decided to completely disinherit his family, he revised his plan to give all his assets to a friend instead. The attorney barely knew the man; he had only met with him twice. The man made the attorney promise not to mention the change to his niece. When the man died four months later, the family challenged the plan in court. After thousands of dollars in legal fees, the matter was finally settled, but no one was happy with the result.

Instead of planning secretly, let your family know your desires, give them all a copy of the plan and have them sign a waiver of the right to contest. Even if not bulletproof, having the written waiver goes a long way toward heading off fighting before it starts.

When 85-year-old Lillian changed her estate plan, she gave a copy to all three of her children. She also gave them a document asking each child to review the documents and waive any right to contest her plan. She explained in writing that she had previously given a substantial amount of property to one of her sons, which would remain his without any offset at her death. She also explained that her other son had been helping her in her business and he had been paid in full for his time, with nothing further due to him at her death, to reduce the possibility that he might seek additional compensation for his services. When she died, the kids followed through with their promise not to contest the plan; her assets were distributed to her three children without any disputes.

3.   *Customize the Estate Plan to Your Unique Circumstances*

Having a "No Contest Clause" provision in a Living Trust, which disinherits a child who files a contest of the estate plan, can also keep family harmony. The child is unlikely to start a fight for fear of being disinherited.

However, such a clause doesn't prevent all fights. In fact, used incorrectly, it can be counterproductive. Adhering to the third principal, customizing the estate plan to each situation, generally avoids most fights before they begin.

Consider a mother who created a Living Trust, leaving all her assets to her two children equally. After creating the Living Trust, her daughter divorced. Worried that her daughter wouldn't have a place to live, the mother took the home out of the trust, and added her daughter as "Joint Tenant" so that, if she died, the home would transfer directly to her daughter.

The mother included a No Contest Clause in her Living Trust, which provided that if anyone filed any contest of the Living Trust, no matter how reasonable the challenge, the contestant would be disinherited. Such a broadly worded No Contest Clause could be disastrous: If the daughter were to defend her right to the house by even responding to a court petition filed by one of her siblings, she would be in violation of the clause and at risk of losing everything. The No Contest Clause should have been drafted to apply only to the sons who might contest the plan, not to the daughter who might need to file court petitions to protect herself and enforce her mother's wishes.

A trust that divides assets equally between two children may not need a No Contest Clause. If the trust does contain such a clause, the trust must be tailored to suit the situation. For example, the mother's Living Trust in the example above should provide that any contest filed with "probable cause" is not a violation of the No Contest Clause and should specifically instruct the Trustee to distribute the home to her daughter.

A customized No Contest Clause won't prevent all fights. For example, even with a No Contest Clause in the Living Trust, children can still make the specific claim that their mother's Living Trust is invalid and should be disregarded because their mother lacked the required capacity to sign it, or because the parent was under the undue influence of another child. As long as the children can pass the "probable cause" legal standard they can begin a battle in court without the risk of losing their inheritance, despite the No Contest Clause. If the facts would cause a reasonable person to believe there is a reasonable likelihood that the contestant is right, that child can start a court battle without worrying about the No Contest Clause. Because the child won't risk disinheritance by filing the court action, the No Contest Clause will fail to deter a child claiming lack of capacity or undue influence.

Avoiding cookie cutter trusts and one-size-fits-all plans can extinguish most disputes before the flames of destruction spread. Rather than including boilerplate provisions, assess the possible controversies and run interference before the fighting starts. To prevent family feuds, identify potential troublemakers and customize the plan to thwart their potential challenges. Fully explore any concerns, and then consider creative ways to address those particular concerns in the written estate plan.

POTENTIAL CONFLICTS AND PROACTIVE SOLUTIONS: EXAMPLES OF HOW TO CUSTOMIZE AN ESTATE PLAN

❖ A "Problem Spouse": Give a conditional gift to a spouse who might challenge the plan. Potential fighting between a surviving spouse and stepchildren can be addressed by giving the surviving spouse a gift of assets in the Living Trust conditioned upon his agreement not to claim any right to other property outside of the Living Trust. He can only receive the trust assets if he agrees in writing not to claim any interest in any of the assets passing outside of the Living Trust.

❖ The "Problem Child": Give a neutral person the power to give certain assets in the Living Trust to a "Problem Child" if the child doesn't act up.

The Problem Child will be on good behavior hoping to receive the trust assets. Now the child has incentive not to create problems because if she does, she won't get the assets.

❖ The Unequal Trust Division: Target the No Contest Clause to the most likely contestant. If parents create a Living Trust that gives one daughter 80% of the assets and another daughter 20%, the Living Trust should have a No Contest Clause that only applies to the daughter receiving the 20%. The daughter receiving 80% of the assets certainly won't be the one to contest so the No Contest Clause doesn't need to apply to her. Dissuade the potentially unhappy daughter from contesting by making the clause only apply to her, allowing the other daughter the right to defend the trust and enforce its terms.

❖ Avoid a Challenge to an Accounting: A beneficiary who only receives a set cash gift should not have the right to see all the books and records of the trust. The estate plan should relieve the Trustee of the duty to account to that beneficiary to head off any potential challenge of the accounting by this beneficiary.

❖ The Priceless Family Heirlooms: To prevent siblings from fighting about family heirlooms, an estate plan should include specific written instructions about who gets what. Alternatively, give a neutral third party the sole and exclusive power to make the final decision if children can't agree on a particular item.

You have a lot of control over what happens *after* you die. By planning your estate properly, you can reduce the chances of family feuds. A thoughtful estate plan can extinguish the flames of a potential dispute before it gets out of control.

> **LIFE LESSONS:**
>
> ❖ *Don't name children as Trustees if the children don't get along. If they fight now, they will fight even more after a parent's death. Putting a neutral party in charge can ensure family harmony.*
>
> ❖ *Carefully use a No-Contest Clause that disinherits a contestant, and consider whether the clause should only apply to the "troublemaker" heir. A well-drafted No Contest Clause, although not always effective, can still dissuade beneficiaries from fighting. It can also, however, cause unforeseen and unwanted results. It is therefore vital to customize the clause to address your particular concerns.*

Talk to your attorney and tax advisor if you have life insurance. Having the right "owner" and "beneficiary" of the policy will determine whether the life insurance proceeds go to the IRS, to your kids or to their creditors.

Critical Fact #10: Protect Life Insurance Proceeds by Holding Life Insurance in an Irrevocable Life Insurance Trust

People mistakenly think that because life insurance with a proper beneficiary designation form avoids probate court, no further planning is needed. Probate, however, isn't the only problem; protection from creditors and from the IRS is critical as well.

Worried about what would happen to her 10-year-old son if she died, Trisha took out a $500,000 life insurance policy and named him as the beneficiary. However, she never planned who would manage the insurance proceeds for her young son. Without proper planning, she won't know where the insurance proceeds will end up if her son gets married and then divorces. Creditors might be able to access the money if her son goes into business and gets sued. How you plan your insurance will determine whether the IRS gets a portion of the proceeds, how the insurance is used, whether it's subject to the reach of creditors and whether the proceeds can grow and pass to the next generation.

People with taxable estates, meaning assets more than their available Exemption, should consider creating an Irrevocable Life Insurance Trust for their life insurance. A properly drafted and administered Irrevocable Life Insurance Trust, sometimes called an "ILIT" for short, will remove the life insurance proceeds from the insured's estate so that the proceeds are not subject to estate tax when the insured dies.

The ILIT will have its own separate tax ID number, meaning that the Trustee of the ILIT will file a separate annual tax return for the trust. The ILIT is basically an instruction manual, which governs the ownership of the insurance and the use of the insurance proceeds if the insured dies. The insured generally won't serve as the Trustee or co-Trustee of the trust; someone independent—i.e., someone who is not a beneficiary—will act as Trustee, but the insured will have the right to fire the Trustee and appoint a new one.

The steps to create and fund the typical ILIT are relatively basic:
1. Once the ILIT is drafted and signed and the tax ID number obtained, the Trustee of the ILIT completes the insurance application and opens a bank account in the name of the ILIT.

2. The insured that created the ILIT gifts cash to the trust and the Trustee deposits the gift into the ILIT bank account.

3. The Trustee generally needs to provide the trust beneficiaries with a letter informing them of the cash gift to the trust and giving them the right to withdraw the cash within a specified time (i.e., 45 days). This notice enables the insured to reduce and sometimes even avoid any gift tax on the gift to the trust.

4. Once the time period in the notice expires, the Trustee pays the insurance premium. Each year, before the premium is due, the insured again gifts money in the trust, the Trustee sends the notification letter to the beneficiaries and, at the expiration of the withdrawal period, pays the premium.

Without the ILIT owning the life insurance, for those who die with assets more than their available Exemption, up to 40 cents of every dollar of the life insurance will potentially go to the IRS instead of to the kids who need it. Owning life insurance in an Irrevocable Trust—and following all the rules—places the proceeds outside the reach of the IRS. When the insured dies, the insurance proceeds are excluded from the decedent's assets, and they are therefore not subject to estate tax. The bottom line: Anyone with an estate that may exceed their available Exemption and be subject to estate tax should consider holding any life insurance in an Irrevocable Trust.

AN ALTERNATIVE TO THE IRREVOCABLE LIFE INSURANCE TRUST; NAME THE LIVING TRUST AS THE BENEFICIARY OF LIFE INSURANCE

Whenever an estate is large enough (over the available Exemption) to be subject to estate tax, an insured should consider owning it in an Irrevocable Trust. If, however, the insurance is not held in an Irrevocable Trust, the insured should at least consider naming the Living Trust as the beneficiary of the life insurance. That way, after the insured dies, the Living Trust can direct the life insurance proceeds.

Naming a Living Trust as the beneficiary of life insurance can protect the insurance proceeds when the Living Trust provides for an ongoing Irrevocable Trust. For example, when a Living Trust instructs the Trustee to fund an ongoing trust, such as a traditional Bypass Trust for a surviving spouse, naming the Living Trust as the beneficiary of the life insurance could enable the Bypass Trust to protect the insurance proceeds from estate tax and potential creditors in case of a lawsuit filed against the surviving spouse.

When a Living Trust instructs the Trustee to fund an ongoing Irrevocable Trust for children (e.g., a Sprinkling Trust, Separate Share Trust or Dynasty Trust), naming the Living Trust as the beneficiary can direct the insurance proceeds into the children's trust, protecting the insurance proceeds. In fact, keeping insurance protected in a Dynasty Trust created under a Living Trust can shield the assets from the reach of unforeseen creditors or a divorcing spouse (who might become a creditor!) for generations to come.

When a large insurance policy will flow into a Living Trust, adding the bells and whistles of special trust provisions that make the children's trust a so-called "fully discretionary" Dynasty Trust means that creditors will have a harder time forcing a distribution from the trust because an independent Trustee will maintain the sole and absolute discretion of whether to make any trust distributions. While not bulletproof (no asset protection is), a well-drafted Dynasty Trust can certainly be a roadblock for creditors.

People often simply name their children on the life insurance Beneficiary Designation, thinking that they will let their children worry about how to protect the insurance proceeds. Unfortunately, the children cannot take the same steps to protect the proceeds that you can because most states don't allow people to set up a creditor-protected trust for themselves. For example, if faced with a lawsuit, an adult child would have a hard time transferring $1 million of insurance proceeds into an Irrevocable Trust, have access to the funds as needed for support and protect it from creditors. However, if the adult child already had all the insurance proceeds in a fully discretionary Irrevocable Trust with an independent Trustee in control, those assets could be protected. After all, it's doubtful that creditors would spend the time and money going to court if they knew that, even if they won, they'd never be able to collect.

With proper planning, insurance can remain protected for future generations. With the wrong planning (or without planning), the insurance could end up in the hands of the IRS, creditors or a divorcing spouse. While all insurance with a proper Beneficiary Designation will avoid probate, naming the right beneficiary can protect the assets for generations to come.

LIFE LESSONS:

Don't automatically name your spouse as the primary beneficiary of your life insurance. Insurance will be distributed according to the instructions contained in a "Beneficiary Designation." Those who don't create an Irrevocable Trust to own the insurance policy often mistakenly name their spouse on the Beneficiary Designation. Instead, consider naming the Living Trust on the Beneficiary Designation. Then, the insurance proceeds can be funded into the Irrevocable Trusts created for a spouse, such as a Bypass Trust or a Disclaimer Trust, and be protected from estate tax when the surviving spouse dies. Naming the Living Trust will also protect the proceeds from Sexy Sue or Don Juan should the surviving spouse re-marry.

Critical Fact #11: Take Steps to Protect (or to Defend Against!) Stepchildren

We no longer live in the era of Ozzie and Harriet. Today's families are more like the families on the TV sitcom "Modern Family"—second marriages and children from both marriages. Today's families need the right plan to protect their children and spouse. Otherwise, stepchildren may end up in a court battle with their stepparents when their biological parent dies or becomes incapacitated.

Couples with "blended families," meaning kids from prior marriages, can be confused: They don't know what to leave to the surviving spouse and what to leave for the children. If they create one joint Living Trust for the sole benefit of the surviving spouse, their respective children may never get a dime. If they create separate Living Trusts for the sole benefit of their respective children, the surviving spouse will be left high and dry.

Estate plans don't need to be all or nothing. Creative estate planning can protect both the surviving spouse and the children from the prior marriage. Avoid analysis paralysis, where you fret and become so overwhelmed at the different options that you don't create any estate plan, by considering three different practical plans for blended families:

Plan #1: Create Separate Living Trusts

Each spouse creating separate Living Trusts with their separate assets works great for couples who don't commingle their money or property. These couples usually

sign a written agreement, either before they marry or afterwards, keeping their finances separate.

Couples who keep their finances separate should always engage a family law attorney and comply with their state laws concerning property rights. Simply "keeping assets separate" may not be legally binding.

Couples who marry later in life and have significant assets and grown children will generally want separate estate plans that leave their assets to their respective children. That way, the stepchildren won't be waiting around until the stepparent dies to receive the assets (sounds terrible, but that's reality!). Instead, the children receive the assets when their parent dies.

For the right couple, keeping assets separate and creating a separate estate plan for each spouse can help preserve family harmony.

> *Separate and Simple:* Stan and Sara each had significant wealth and married late in life. When Stan died and he left all his assets to his children, they remained close to their stepmother long after their father died. The children received their inheritance when their dad died so they didn't need to worry that their stepmother would use up all the money, leaving nothing to them. Stan's separate estate plan created such family harmony that the stepmom is like a second mom to the children and is "Grammy" to the grandchildren. With money out of the picture, their family harmony is surviving through the generations.

LIFE LESSONS:

When each spouse has a separate estate plan, be sure to identify the spouse and all the children and stepchildren in the estate plan. If either the spouse or children are not provided for in the plan, expressly identify the ones not provided for and "disinherit" them. Although it sounds harsh to "disinherit" someone, being direct and clear can be critical. Otherwise, under certain state laws, the omitted children or spouse could claim they were omitted by mistake, and therefore entitled to part of the assets. If you are concerned that one of the children or your spouse will challenge the plan, consider including a gift to the person and a provision, called a No Contest Clause, that the person will lose the inheritance completely if the person challenges the plan

Plan #2: Create a Joint Living Trust and Treat All Children Equally

Kate was not the stereotypical Sexy Sue. Yes, she was the second spouse, but she was married to Clyde for 42 years. She had two children, Clyde had two children and they had one child from their marriage to each other. They created one joint Living Trust, giving *all* the children an equal share of their estate. Because both of them were equally close and connected to all the kids, they treated the children as if they were all children of their marriage.

Creating one joint Living Trust worked well for Kate and Clyde because the estate plan contained sufficient protections and safeguards for the kids, including a provision that if Clyde changed the plan after Kate died, certain offsets would assure that all the kids receive an equal share of the estate.

For another blended family, the Living Trust failed to include safeguards, proving disastrous for the kids. The couple created one joint Living Trust. All of the assets in the trust were to benefit the surviving spouse for life. When the surviving spouse later died, all of the assets were to be divided equally among all of their children.

What they did not foresee is that after one spouse died, the surviving spouse fell in love, remarried, and left all of the assets in the Living Trust to the new spouse, disinheriting all of the children. All of the children were treated equally— none of them received a dime. The problem wasn't that the couple decided to have one joint Living Trust. The problem was that the Living Trust should have been drafted differently. In light of the goals, the Living Trust should have provided that the deceased spouse's assets would be put into an Irrevocable Trust for the surviving spouse, with protections for the children about the use of the assets.

Creating a joint Living Trust and treating all the children equally can keep family harmony when a couple has been married a long time and each spouse feels emotionally connected to all of the children. Be sure that the joint trust is drafted properly, considering what powers the surviving spouse should have to modify the trust, the duties to give financial information to the children after a spouse dies, and the ability (or restrictions) of the surviving spouse to spend all the money in the trust.

Plan #3: Use Life Insurance to Create a Fair Result for Stepchildren

One couple created a Living Trust to benefit the two children of their current marriage, leaving nothing for the children from their prior marriages. They transferred

their home, savings accounts, rental properties and business into their joint Living Trust. Then, they purchased life insurance policies for their respective children. The Living Trust will give all of the trust assets to the two children of their marriage. The life insurance on the husband will go to his children from a previous marriage when he dies. The life insurance on the wife will go to her children from a previous marriage when she dies.

Using life insurance for the children of a prior marriage simplifies the Living Trust, which would generally give all the assets to the surviving spouse and then to the children of the couple's marriage. The deceased spouse won't worry about protecting the remaining assets in the trust for the children, knowing that the surviving spouse is the biological parent of the children. Most importantly, each spouse will have peace of mind knowing that the biological children will have already received their inheritance when that spouse dies.

The life insurance guarantees that children from prior marriages receive an inheritance at the death of their parent, without having to wait for a stepparent to die. It also alleviates stress for the stepparent: No one will be looking over the stepparent's shoulder wondering how the money is being spent.

Using a joint Living Trust for the children of the current marriage and life insurance for the children from prior marriages also minimizes the potential for fighting. The structure builds an order, and confidence that everyone's needs will be met. The surviving spouse can be given greater latitude about the use of the assets, the children of the current marriage know that their parents have provided for them, and the children will receive assets when their biological parent dies.

Families come in all sizes and shapes, and so should their estate plans. Creative but simple planning can be the key to your family's harmony.

Critical Fact #12: Review Your Estate Plan

Today's biggest estate planning problem is the failure to create a plan. The second biggest mistake is not reviewing it.

> *Anna Nicole's Baby:* Anna Nicole Smith signed a Will leaving her entire estate to her son and specifically disinheriting all future born children. Years later, she had a baby girl and shortly afterwards her 20-year-old-son died, allegedly of a drug overdose. Anna never amended her Will

to reflect her son's death or her daughter's birth. Amending her Will would have ensured that her estate went to her daughter, saving tens of thousands of dollars and years of fighting in court.

Beneficiary Dies: Stuart died with a Will. However, the person he named in the Will had died long ago, and he had never updated it. Instead of choosing his own beneficiaries, the court chose them for him after his death.

Retirement Accounts Not Properly Accounted For: Sam died with his ex-spouse still named as the beneficiary of his retirement accounts. Fortunately, under the law of his residency, California, the dissolution of the marriage invalidated the Beneficiary Designation. Unfortunately, because Sam didn't name anyone else as a beneficiary, the court handled the distribution of the retirement accounts. He did not get any say in who received his hard-earned retirement accounts. To make matters worse, rather than being paid annually over the life expectancy of the beneficiary, the income taxes on the full value of the retirement accounts were due up front.

The Unnecessary Bypass Trust: Bill and Cynthia' plan required that the assets of the first spouse to die be put into a traditional Bypass Trust. When Bill died, his assets were transferred into the Bypass Trust, creating tons of hassle for Cynthia, who had to give a copy of the Bypass Trust provisions to her stepchildren and provide an accounting to them annually. Had they reviewed their plan, they might have given all the assets to the surviving spouse in a more flexible and simple trust. They didn't need the Bypass Trust to minimize estate tax because they had a small estate and the high Exemption under the Taxpayer Relief Act already eliminated estate tax. Further, after 50 years of marriage, the added hassle of the Bypass Trust far outweighed any protection it provided.

After you sign your estate plan and re-title your assets in the name of the trust, review your estate plan every year or two. It is especially important to review your plan after any major changes in your life. Make sure your plan is flexible, and consider giving a trusted friend or advisor the power as an Independent Trustee to change your plan for you, in response to any changes in the law, if you are unable to do so. Tax time is the perfect time to review your plan; you will already be spending time examining your finances and any changes in your life. Don't make any changes on your original signed estate plan; instead, sign a new document to amend your

Estate Plan. While you are talking to your tax preparer, consider whether you have had any material changes in your life and whether your estate plan is up to date by referring to the Estate Plan Review Checklist below.

Once you sign your estate plan, you will be responsible for scheduling periodic review meetings with your attorney to discuss any changes in the law that would necessitate changes to your plan. A stale, out-of-date estate plan can be as bad, if not worse, than not having a plan at all.

ESTATE PLAN REVIEW CHECKLIST

Review your estate plan every few years or if you have experienced major changes in your life that could affect your plan. Refer to the following checklist when you review your estate plan.

❖ **Assets outside the trust**. Do I have assets outside of my Living Trust that should be governed by my trust (i.e., did I forget to put my home back into the Living Trust after refinancing it or have I purchased assets after creating or revising my Living Trust that I have not yet put into the Living Trust)?

❖ **Life insurance beneficiary.** Have I properly named a beneficiary for my life insurance—both a primary beneficiary and a backup?

❖ **Retirement accounts beneficiary.** Have I properly named a beneficiary for my retirement accounts—both a primary beneficiary and a backup?

❖ **Life changes.** Do I need to reflect any personal life changes in my Living Trust (i.e., marriage, divorce, birth of a child, change in assets or income, move to a new state, etc.)?

❖ **Persons named in plan.** Do I want to change the people I named in my estate plan to manage all of my assets, make my health care decisions and/or care for my children?

❖ **Gifts to charity.** Do I want to make any gifts to charities that are not already in my Living Trust?

❖ **Aging children.** Do the ongoing trusts for my children need to be changed now that they are older?

❖ **New children or grandchildren.** Are all my children and grandchildren named in the Living Trust?

❖ **Outdated bypass trust.** Will my Living Trust create income tax issues that can be avoided by changing the Living Trust (i.e., do I have a Bypass Trust that I don't need or want)?

Critical Fact #13: Special Alert for California Property Owners: Avoid Higher Property Tax After You Die with Proper Estate Planning

With education and planning, California property tax owners can prevent higher property tax when they die and help ensure that their loved ones can afford to keep the property. Otherwise, the inheritor of California real property upon a death may not be able to afford the higher property tax.

> *Property Transferred To Corporation:* Stella didn't know what not to do: During her lifetime, she transferred all her real property into a corporation to protect it from creditors. When she died, the property taxes skyrocketed, recalculated based on the higher value of the property at the date of her death. Stella's son is now shackled with the higher property taxes.

> *House Transferred To Partner:* Robert didn't know what to do: He lived with his partner for 20 years and left his house to his partner. When he died, property taxes doubled, based on the reassessed value of the property at Robert's date of death. With the higher property taxes, Robert's partner could no longer afford the house.

> *Everything Left To Children:* Daniel and Cindy didn't know what to do: They created a Living Trust leaving everything equally to their two adult children. When Daniel and Cindy died, each son took title to half of the home, and then one son sold his half to his brother. Property taxes skyrocketed.

You can avoid property reassessment and increasing property taxes after you die. If Stella had not transferred her property to a corporation, her son would have paid the same low property taxes she had been paying, adjusted annually by the lesser of 2 percent or the state's inflation rate according to Proposition 13 (the "inflation index"). Had Robert and his partner become Registered Domestic Partners or married, or co-owned the property, Robert's partner would have paid the same low property tax that Robert had been paying plus the inflation index. Had Daniel and Cindy left their home to their one son who wanted it and left other assets of equal value to their other son, the son who inherited the home would have paid the same low property tax that his parents had been paying plus the inflation index.

Always consult an attorney or tax advisor after a death to determine what action is needed to address property tax on California real property. When parents leave a house to their two children and one child wants all of the house, the Trustee of a trust may be able to borrow against the house, put the loan proceeds into a trust bank account and distribute the home to one child and the loan proceeds (cash) of equal value to the other child. This method of trust distribution, called a "non pro rata" distribution, along with filing a parent-child exclusion form with the assessor, may have avoided property tax reassessment for Daniel and Cindy's son in the example above.

Knowing the rules makes all the difference. For California property owners, death creates a "change of ownership" that triggers increased property taxes, unless an exception applies, some of which require post-death paperwork to claim:

A FEW EXCEPTIONS WHEN PROPERTY VALUES ARE NOT REASSESSED AT DEATH

❖ Spouses and Registered Domestic Partners who leave their real property to the surviving spouse/registered domestic partner.

❖ Parents who leave their primary residence to their children.

❖ Parents who leave up to $1 million of assessed value (or $2 million for a married couple) of other real property, such as second homes and investment property, to their children.

❖ Grandparents who leave real property to grandchildren, if the grandchildren's parents are deceased.

❖ Co-owners who meet the requirements of Section 62.3 of the Revenue and Taxation Code, as explained below.

Because property tax laws change frequently, and the consequences can be costly, owners of California real estate need to stay abreast of the laws that will affect their property. Co-owners of real property need to know how much the surviving owners will pay in property tax if one co-owner dies. Otherwise, the surviving owner may not be able to afford the property tax.

Under current law, planning has gotten easier for couples who co-own their primary residence. They no longer have to be married or Registered Domestic Partners to avoid property tax reassessment when one spouse/partner dies. Under the 2013 Co-tenancy Rule, AB 1700, which amended Section 62.3 of the Revenue and Taxation Code, a surviving co-owner can avoid a property tax increase upon death by:

1. Owning the property with the words "Joint Tenants" or "Tenants in Common" on the title.

2. Living in the property as their primary residence for at least one year before a death.

3. Leaving the property to the other co-owner at death.
4. Signing a certain document after a death attesting to the facts above.

California property owners who fail to follow the simple rules trigger an expensive and needless reassessment of their property. Educated property owners reap the benefits of Proposition 13, which keeps property taxes down. When creating an estate plan, make sure anyone who inherits California real property can receive the property without property tax reassessment, and determine what property tax forms are need after a death.

Spouses are lucky. If Craig dies and passes his real property to his wife Susan, the transfer of the property to Susan will qualify as a spousal exclusion, and Susan will pay the same property taxes that she would have paid had Craig not died. On the other hand, if Craig transfers his real property to a grandson when Craig's son, the grandson's father, is still living, the property will be reassessed because transfers to a grandson only qualify for a property tax exclusion if the grandson's parent who is the child of the grandfather is deceased. In other words, property can't skip over a *living* child to a grandchild and pass free of property tax reassessment.

Similarly, if Craig transfers real property to a trust and if the Trustee of the trust has discretion to distribute trust assets to a grandson, 100% of the real property in the trust will be reassessed if Craig skips over his living child who is the parent of his grandson. Craig could have avoided the reassessment by giving his son the real property and leaving other assets to his grandson.

Children who swap assets after their parents die also frequently trigger higher property taxes. If Edith's Living Trust instructs the Trustee to distribute the Tahoe cabin to her daughter and the Stinson Beach house to her son, the kids can't exchange properties without a complete reassessment to the current fair market value of the property. Had Edith's Living Trust instructed the Trustee to distribute all the Living Trust assets to her daughter and son in equal shares on a so-called "pro rata or non pro rata basis," as determined by the Trustee, she would have averted a reassessment of the trust property. Then, the Trustee could consult with the children to determine which property each child wants and avoid the reassessment. As long as they each get an equal share of the trust assets, the makeup of each share won't affect property taxes. The parent-child exclusion from property tax assets avoids a reassessment of both properties.

Sometimes property tax reassessment upon death can be avoided through an action known as a "**Qualified Disclaimer**." A disclaimer is a written document indicating

that the signor does not want the asset that was given to her. The document must be signed and delivered to the Trustee of a trust within nine months of the right to receive the asset. In other words, if someone dies, then within nine months of the death, and before receiving any benefit from the trust asset, a trust beneficiary can sign a document that complies with the law, called a Qualified Disclaimer, informing the Trustee that the beneficiary does not intend to accept the asset. The Trustee would then need to distribute the asset as if the person disclaiming were deceased, and the asset would pass to the next beneficiary named in the trust.

Assume that Bill names his daughter Sandra and Sandra's children as the beneficiaries of his Living Trust, which holds mostly California real property. Because Sandra's children do not qualify for an exclusion while Sandra is living, the grandchildren can disclaim their interest in the Living Trust. Without the disclaimer, 100% of the real property in the trust would be reassessed to its current fair market value. When someone forms a Living Trust and mistakenly names a beneficiary who does not qualify for an exclusion, the beneficiary of the trust can sometimes prevent a full reassessment of the real property by disclaiming an interest, curing a potentially costly mistake.

California property owners must understand how Proposition 13 affects them in life and death. Good planning can determine whether your loved ones will be able to afford to keep your home and other real property or whether they will be forced to sell it.

LIFE LESSONS:

Discuss real property with the intended beneficiaries in advance of preparing a Living Trust. Sometimes one child wants the real property and another child does not. If the Living Trust is properly drafted, the Trustee will be able to distribute the real property to the child who wants it without the property being reassessed and subject to increased property taxes. If one child wants the home, for example, you can draft the Living Trust with a special gift of the home to that child, leaving other assets to the other children; as long as the proper forms are filed, property taxes will not increase upon death.

Critical Fact #14: Special Alert for California Residents (and Residents of Other Community Property States): The Blessing and the Curse—You Must Understand How Community Property Laws Affect You, Your Assets, and Your Spouse

Not understanding California's unique community property rules can devastate a surviving spouse. Creating a written agreement between spouses can be even more dangerous. If you own or were gifted any assets before your marriage, you must understand how community property laws affect you in the event of both divorce and death. The following anecdote highlights the importance of understanding California community property law:

> *Transmutation Trouble:* Stan came into his marriage to Emily with a great deal of money, including a huge house with a mortgage. He paid down the mortgage during their 10-year marriage and spent a lot of time wisely investing his money.
>
> Not understanding California's community property/separate property law, Stan signed a "Transmutation Agreement" to make everything they owned "community property." He signed the agreement as part of his estate plan, which specified what Emily would receive if he were to die as well as what would happen if Emily died first.
>
> He did not sign the Transmutation Agreement anticipating a divorce, but to ensure that, if Emily died, he would save income tax on the sale of the appreciated assets. He had heard that in the event of death community property, as opposed to separate property, receives favorable tax treatment via a full step up in income tax basis.
>
> However, Emily didn't die. Two years after signing the Transmutation Agreement, Emily filed for divorce, and Emily wanted "her half" of all the assets. Stan wanted to reclaim all of his assets, saying that they were his "separate property" because they were his assets before he married Emily.
>
> In court, Stan argued that the "Transmutation Agreement" only applied if he or Emily died, not if they divorced. The judge disagreed and ruled that all of the assets Stan owned before he married Emily

were now "community property" under California law. Accordingly, half of it belonged to Emily upon divorce. Understanding the legal effect of the Transmutation Agreement (and not signing it!) would have saved Stan the $5 million that went to Emily).

Under California law, community property is treated drastically different than separate property, upon both death and divorce. You can avoid Stan's mistake by following these steps:

❖ Obtain legal advice from an attorney who specializes in family law (that means an attorney who handles divorce matters) to determine whether your assets are "separate property" or "community property" under the state law where you reside. Consider whether to sign an agreement that confirms or changes the character of your assets. Do not sign any agreement that attempts to change "separate property" to "community property" without consulting with a family law attorney.

❖ Consider whether to hire two different attorneys rather than having one attorney represent both of you in preparing your estate plan.

❖ If you decide to engage one attorney for both of you, understand the potential conflict of interest the attorney will have in fairly representing both of you. Get examples of how the attorney's advice could adversely impact one of you.

❖ Consider creating a separate estate plan for "separate property" or a Living Trust that offers you exclusive control over your separate property as the sole Trustee of a "separate property trust," which can still be governed by the joint trust.

Community property laws can have unintended consequences to those without knowledge. You now have the knowledge to create the right estate plan that will protect your loved ones and your assets.

THE TAKE-AWAY FROM STEP #3

When you take a car to a mechanic, you don't need to know everything about how your engine works. Similarly, when you begin your estate planning, you don't need to become a walking encyclopedia on estate planning. You just need to be aware of the critical facts explored in Step #3. With an understanding of the basics, you are ready for Step #4.

STEP #4:

GET IT DONE! DECIDE WHETHER TO DO IT YOURSELF OR HIRE AN ATTORNEY

Congratulations! You have completed the Boot Camp and have a basic understanding of important facts to help you draft a thoughtful estate plan. Your first decision is whether you are going to complete the planning yourself or hire an attorney.

Congratulations! You have completed the Boot Camp and have a basic understanding of important facts to help you draft a thoughtful estate plan. Your first decision is whether you are going to complete the planning yourself or hire an attorney. If you want to complete your estate plan yourself, now is the time to begin. If you decide to hire an attorney, call and set up your initial consultation this week. An attorney will generally need about two weeks to prepare a draft of the estate plan for your review. Either way, you should be able to sign your estate plan in less than 30 days.

If your assets are under the value that can pass without going through probate court (in 2014, California residents can pass $150,000, excluding certain assets such as

IRAs and life insurance, without probate court) and you do not own your own home or have any other real estate, and especially if you are relatively young, you may be a good candidate for preparing your own plan. Similarly, if your assets are all held in (i) retirement accounts, (ii) pay on death accounts and (iii) joint tenancy (no matter what the value), you also could consider preparing an estate plan without hiring an attorney.

Using an experienced attorney can provide helpful feedback about the right person to put in charge of your assets (as Trustee) and to care for your children (as guardian), and how to minimize family feuding after you die. The attorney can help ensure that you have not overlooked critical issues and provide help in special circumstances such as estate planning for couples with a second marriage or those with a taxable estate. Establishing a relationship with a trusted attorney your loved ones can call after your demise can also give you peace of mind.

Before making a decision about whether to do it yourself or hire an attorney, you will need to know the important issues that might be overlooked on your own, what can go wrong in hiring an attorney, what to ask an attorney, and what it costs.

LIFE LESSONS:

Determine whether you need an estate plan by consulting an attorney. With so many factors to consider and constantly changing laws, don't jump to your own conclusions. Chances are you, or your loved ones, will discover you are wrong when it's too late to do anything about it. Honest attorneys (they do exist) will tell you whether you should hire an attorney to prepare your estate plan.

The Most Frequently Overlooked Issues with a Do-It-Yourself Estate Plan

People who don't seek professional advice often leave their families with a host of problems. Most people don't know what they don't know, and they therefore don't know what questions to ask. Estate planning is technical, and most people don't have the specific skills and knowledge to create a plan themselves.

For example, failure to draft a Will or Living Trust can lead to family feuding:

Not Worth The Paper It's Written On: Sally believed she had a plan that bequeathed her house to her daughter. She had a written agreement with her husband clearly indicating that she intended to leave her home to her daughter. When she died, her daughter was left with a big mess to clean up. Why? Because her plan didn't include a Living Trust or a Will, only the written agreement with her husband that they would each leave their assets to their respective children.

Sally should have transferred her house into a Living Trust and intentionally disinherited her husband, whom she had only married four years before her death. If she had done this, the house would have passed to her daughter without controversy and without the time and expense of court proceedings. Unfortunately, Sally didn't know what she didn't know, and therefore didn't know what questions to ask. Sally's daughter ended up in a court battle with her stepfather, who claimed that under California law he was entitled to half of the house.

Drafting a Will without specific instructions on management and distribution of your home can also lead to unnecessary and costly court battles after your death:

Holes in Holographic Will: Cynthia drafted a written plan, but it wasn't sufficient to avoid a court battle. Cynthia was leaving on a trip and decided to handwrite a note dictating what should happen if she died. At the top of the page, she wrote, "Will." She signed and dated it and put it in her drawer. In the instructions, she wrote that if she died, her husband could live in the house. She instructed that, when he died, the house be distributed to her daughter.

Tragically, Cynthia had a stroke at the airport and died. Her handwritten Will only added to her family's devastation: Cynthia's husband, Harold, was not the father of her daughter, and the two spent the year after Cynthia's death fighting in court. Harold already owned half the house, and Cynthia owned the other half. The Will indicated that Harold had the right to her half of the house for his life; in other words, he could live there until he died.

Within three months of Cynthia's unexpected death, the fighting began. Her daughter claimed that the house was built on an eroding hillside that needed repairs. Harold disagreed and was not willing to spend any money on the repairs. If he didn't, the daughter argued, she would lose her inheritance—the house would be a pile of dirt at the bottom of the eroding hill.

Cynthia's estate plan was doomed from the beginning. Too many factors were left unconsidered: whether her daughter, rather than her husband, should be left in charge, or, alternatively, whether to buy life insurance to leave to her daughter, and bequeath the house directly to her husband without any strings or restrictions attached.

Cynthia knew that a handwritten, signed, dated and witnessed document met the requirements of a valid Will (called a **Holographic Will**). However, she didn't know how to divide her assets to keep family harmony. Lacking the knowledge to ask the right questions, Cynthia left her family to fight it out in court.

Couples could easily neglect to add the assurances in their plan to prevent one spouse from changing the plan without notice to the other.

Sneaky Husband: Dan and Ann created a written estate plan that allowed one spouse to change the plan "with notice to the Trustee." A few months before Dan died, he updated the plan, leaving all of his share to children of his prior marriage and nothing to his wife. He never told her. His wife didn't find out about it until after his death. She challenged the plan in court and lost. The court said that the changed plan was enforceable because their written plan did not require notice to the other spouse for a change to be effective. Under the state law where Dan and Ann lived, Dan's amendment was effective, and Ann was out of luck (and assets.) A do-it-yourself plan can easily ail to provide the protection couples need and want.

Parents also leave assets to their children incorrectly because they don't understand all the options. Some parents without much money leave their money in trusts for their children, causing too many administrative expenses and hassle for too little money. Other parents leave money directly to their children when keeping it in a trust would better safeguard the money from creditors and ex-spouses. Owners of large estates with responsible children often forget that a lifetime trust for children protects the assets from factors beyond the children's control, such as creditors (e.g., someone who might sue the child when the damage from a car accident exceeds the insurance coverage). Parents with young children often don't know whether to leave the money in separate funds for each child—which might not leave enough to a sick or needy child—or in one pot for all the children to use as needed, without keeping track of whether the children receive the same amount of money.

Do-it-yourself plans often fail to address the unique goals of the family. It's difficult to consider and avoid potential mistakes in advance, but, when they occur, they are extremely costly, and often leave survivors feuding and fighting in court.

Hiring an Attorney: What Can Go Wrong

Finding an attorney is easy. Finding the right one is harder. To achieve your desired outcome, you have to choose an estate planning attorney carefully.

You can ask neighbors and friends for a referral to an estate planning attorney. Your neighbors and friends might love and highly recommend their attorney. But those attorneys might not have the expertise in estate planning you need. You want more than a personable attorney; you want an attorney who has the education and experience for your situation. You want an estate planning specialist.

Rather than asking neighbors and friends for a referral, call your state bar association and ask for the name of a specialist in your area. Many states such as California have specialization certifications for estate planning attorneys, which can provide some assurance of the attorney's expertise and experience in estate planning. Alternatively, ask your financial advisor or CPA. They will often know an attorney they have worked with, and can attest to the attorney's competency.

Once you have the names of potential attorney candidates, log on to the website for your State Bar Association. There, you can input the names of the prospective attorneys, learn what school they attended, determine if they specialize in estate planning and how long they have practiced law and, most importantly, discover whether they have any disciplinary proceedings against them.

ATTENTION: Resources for California Residents:

❖ *Call the California State Bar for pamphlets, referrals to attorneys and other valuable—and free—information: http://www.calbar.ca.gov/Public/LawyerReferralServicesLRS.aspx.*

❖ *Contact Lawyer Referral Services at 866-442-2529, 866-44-CA-LAW (toll free in California) or 415-538-2250 (from outside California).*

❖ *LawHelpCA.org helps people of low and moderate incomes find free legal information and legal aid programs in their communities. Choose a topic on their website to find resources, including general information, information on your legal rights, and legal aid organizations.*

❖ *Local bar associations in various counties throughout California can assist with finding an attorney. Certified referral services help you consult with an attorney for a modest fee, sometimes as little as $30-$50. For example, the Lawyer Referral and Information Service (LRIS) of the Los Angeles County Bar Association is a nonprofit public service that allows members of the public to find a qualified attorney and obtain general information about common legal issues. Accessing information through the LRIS and getting a referral to an attorney are both free. Information from the LRIS website: All LRIS attorneys charge fees. LRIS attorneys do not provide free, pro bono legal services. Every LRIS attorney has proven that he or she is qualified in a particular area of law practice and has met many qualifications standards. The LRIS can refer clients to an attorney in just about every area of law practice and in many different language and location requirements (limited to Los Angeles County). Their phone number is (213) 243-1525, Monday through Friday, 8:30 am to 5:00 pm).*

Once you have a referral, it's time to prepare for the initial meeting. Many attorneys will provide an initial consultation for free or for a nominal fee. If you have completed Steps #1 - #3 of this Guide, you have all the preliminary information you need. Bring your list of assets and your estate planning goals to your consultation, along with a list of the seven most critical questions described below.

The Seven Most Critical Questions to Ask an Attorney

Question #1: What percentage of your law practice is estate planning, trusts, and probate?

You want to engage a true expert who understands the intricacies and complexities of estate planning law and has practical experience in handling trust administration after a death. Generally, an attorney who teaches estate planning to other attorneys, is a leader in the field and focuses his or her practice on estate planning is more likely to have the level of experience needed to address the highly technical issues that will affect your estate plan.

Many attorneys take on all types of cases. They may appear in court handling a traffic ticket one day, meet with clients about a divorce the next morning, and craft an estate plan that afternoon. Attorneys who split their focus between different areas of practice may be less able to provide the maximum value for any single task. By retaining a lawyer who focuses solely on drafting wills, creating trusts, and handling other estate, probate, and trust matters, you maximize the chance that the attorney has the necessary expertise to draft a proper estate plan for your unique circumstances.

Question #2: Are you a "Certified Specialist" in estate planning?

Some states, like California, North Carolina and Louisiana to name a few, are unique in that the State Bar has a certification program that helps determine whether an attorney is qualified to prepare your estate plan. In the legal community, being a Certified Specialist in estate planning, trust, and probate law by a Board of Legal Specialization is akin to being a board certified physician in the medical community. It provides assurance from the State Bar that a lawyer has met certain necessary standards establishing competency. In addition to annual educational requirements, a Certified Specialist generally must complete a rigorous examination, meet minimum experience requirements, complete hours of high level classes, and be the subject of peer review by lawyers. Moreover, Certified Specialists must re-certify every few years to ensure that their skills and knowledge are up-to-date. This allows Certified Specialists to incorporate the latest legal options into their estate planning work for clients. In states that offer a certification program, the skill and knowledge requirements often set Certified Specialists apart from other non-certified lawyers.

Question #3: Will a senior partner or a new attorney handle my case?

Every law firm handles cases differently. Depending on the size of the firm, the attorney you originally interact with may not be the one who ultimately performs the

actual legal work on your case. Find out who will be assigned to your case and whether that attorney has the experience you desire. One woman hired an attorney, but after the initial meeting never again communicated with that attorney. A new and inexperienced associate was assigned to her matter, leaving her feeling insecure and duped.

Question #4: What will be included in the scope of the estate planning services?

Once you are confident that your attorney has the needed level of expertise, it is critical to understand exactly what services will be provided for you. Failure to understand what an attorney will or will not do as part of the attorney's services can mean the difference between an effective estate plan and one that leaves you vulnerable.

> *Mother's Work is Never Done:* Dave's mother had a Living Trust naming Dave as sole beneficiary. The mother never transferred her $1 million dollar bank account into the trust. Instead she held that account as Joint Tenants with Dave's brother. When Dave's mother died, the $1 million went to his brother, rather than to Dave. When one person on the title of a joint tenancy account dies, the account passes directly to the other person on the title. Because Dave's brother was the person on the title, he acquired the money, while Dave received nothing. Dave's mother misunderstood the scope of the services provided by her attorney. She never understood it was her responsibility, not her lawyer's, to re-title all her assets.

In estate planning, creating a trust is only Act One. Creating a trust sets the instructions and the scene; transferring assets into that trust is the critical closing act that completes the story. Both acts are essential, and it is important to know from the outset which tasks the attorney will handle and which tasks you will need to handle yourself.

In general, the attorney will draft the Living Trust. However, whether the attorney will transfer individual assets into the Living Trust depends on the written agreement between the attorney and the client, called an **Engagement Agreement**. In some cases, it may be more cost effective for the client to handle the trust transfers, in which case you'll want to make sure that the attorney provides the needed instructions. Without instructions, you might not transfer the assets correctly, which can be as bad as not transferring them at all.

You never want to be surprised at the exact moment when the plan is most needed. Clarify the scope of work with your attorney from the outset and ensure that you are aware of anything that you will need to do yourself after the attorney's work is complete.

Question #5: What are your fees?

Of course, the cost of your attorney may be a factor in your decision. Ensuring that you are aware of the fees that will be charged and avoiding "sticker shock" make the process less stressful. The drafting of certain plans can easily be charged on a flat-fee basis, while other plans need to be billed hourly. If you have a modest net worth and are not married, a flat-fee plan may meet your needs. Your goals will be straightforward, and you'll only need one to two hours of conference time with your attorney. Alternatively, if you have a large net worth or a more unique family situation (i.e., a second marriage or a wide variety of beneficiaries), you might need numerous meetings to solidify your goals; hourly billing is more appropriate in this scenario.

When comparing fees, consider the experience level of the attorney as well as the overall scope of services offered. One attorney may offer a low fee, but the actual services provided may be limited in scope. Similarly, attorneys who do not specialize in estate planning may offer lower fees, but they may be unfamiliar with some details of the work, increasing the risk of mistakes. After a death, there are no "do overs" with an estate plan. If an inexperienced attorney makes a mistake or if some aspect of the work—such as transferring assets into a trust—is not completed, that mistake may have permanent ramifications. The money you "save" by using the lawyer with the lowest fee may well end up being eclipsed by the legal fees that may ultimately be required to deal with mistakes made by that "inexpensive" lawyer. Evaluate all these factors when comparing attorney fees for an estate plan.

Question #6 (For Yourself): Does the attorney explain the law in a clear and understandable way?

Many legal issues are naturally complex. However, your lawyer should be able to break everything down for you so that you fully understand what you are signing. This also ensures that the ramifications of the plan do not surprise family members down the road.

Question #7 (For Yourself): Do you feel comfortable talking and working with this attorney?

Estate planning is a personal matter. It often includes discussions about long-term wishes, burial plans, unique family relationships, and more. Estate planning often requires updates to account for various life changes, such as new marriages,

divorce, new children, new purchases, etc. You might therefore develop an ongoing relationship with your estate-planning attorney. For these reasons, it is important to feel comfortable interacting with your attorney.

Your attorney should make you feel welcome and should clearly explain how the process works. If you are often confused while talking with your attorney, or if you struggle to communicate with your attorney, then consider finding a more compatible lawyer.

What does Estate Planning Cost? (Including Resources for Free or Low-Cost Plans)

When it comes to estate planning, cheaper is not always better. Extremely cheap estate planning commonly means inadequate, cookie-cutter documents that will not meet your unique goals. The cost of a first-rate estate plan is far less than the cost after death when inadequate planning leads to issues.

Many attorneys charge a flat rate for an estate plan, generally ranging from $2,500 to $10,000. This rate depends on many factors, including the value of the assets, the experience of the attorney, and the complexity of the situation. For example, planning for someone with a second marriage and children from a prior marriage will be more expensive than planning an estate for someone who is not married and has no children. The rate for creating Durable Powers of Attorney, Health Care Directives, and Wills is generally in the range of $1,000 to $1,500. Some attorneys will bill their clients on an hourly basis, instead of a flat rate. Others will have a combination flat rate and hourly fee. Many attorneys will even offer their services pro bono or free to those in need.

Most people are naturally fee sensitive. No one wants to get gouged. Nevertheless, beware of cheap estate plans. A Living Trust is a service that requires expertise, sensitivity, and skill. If a fee seems too good to be true, it probably is.

If you cannot afford an estate plan and need a Living Trust and Durable Power of Attorney, some counties offer free legal services. Look in your phone book for options or call your local County Bar Association where you reside. Also, ask an attorney if she provides free legal services to those in need—many do.

ATTENTION CALIFORNIA RESIDENTS: Special Resources

❖ *Free California Will Form: California is unique in that if offers a "statutory" form for a Will that includes complete instructions. If all you need is a simple Will rather than a Living Trust, you don't need to pay anything. Visit the California State Bar website at* www.calbar.ca.gov *and print the California Will form and instructions at no charge.*

❖ *California Advance Health Care Directive: Californians can obtain an Advance Health Care Directive easily and without an attorney. You can print a free Advance Health Care Directive that includes instructions free of charge at* http://ag.ca.gov/consumers/pdf/AHCDS1.pdf. *Most doctors' offices also provide free Advanced Health Care Directives. The California Medical Association offers a wealth of information about Advance Health Care Directives on its website, along with a link to obtain forms for a nominal fee:* http://www.cmanet.org/about/patient-resources/end-of-life-issues/advance-directives. *To order an Advance Health Care Directive kit (offered in both English and Spanish) call the California Medical Association at the Main Switchboard: (800) 786-4262; fax them at (916) 551-2036; or order online:* http://www.cmanet.org/resource-library/detail.dT?item=advance-health-care-directive-kit-english*

How to Keep Signed Documents Safe

Whether you've created your own estate plan or hired an attorney, you should maintain the original signed documents in a safe place. Having an estate plan will be of little help if nobody can find it.

Keep both the original and a copy in a safe place. You should also keep an electronic PDF version on your computer so that you can transmit it to your advisors easily; if you buy or sell your home, you can easily e-mail a copy of your documents to the escrow officer.

Sometimes people leave their signed documents with their attorney. However, unless you want to be wedded to your attorney for life, don't let the drafting attorney keep the original. Instead, keep the original in a safe deposit box at a bank or in a

fireproof safe at home. Additionally, you should give a copy to the person you name as Trustee. Always let the Trustee know where you keep the original, because the Trustee will need it. Lastly, because you should review your plan regularly, keep copies of your estate plan in your files at home for easy reference.

The point of an estate plan is to retain control, so be sure that you are in possession of all of your original estate planning documents and that you have copies at hand for easy reference.

THE FINAL TAKE-AWAY:

Like people, estate plans come in all shapes and sizes. Each estate plan must fit the unique circumstances and intentions of the estate owners. If you do not have a lot of assets, and you don't have particularly unique or complex concerns, a simple Will might suffice. If you have a larger estate, or if you have a second spouse or special concerns about your children, you might appreciate the expert advice of a lawyer who is an estate planning Certified Specialist—not only during planning but to support your family afterwards.

If you decide to consult with a lawyer, bring this 4-Step Action Guide to your meeting. If you have followed the 4-Step Action Guide, you will know your goals, understand the critical basic facts, and have a good idea whether you need an attorney for advice and drafting.

You are now ready to complete your estate plan. Congratulations on taking the steps needed to protect your family and safeguard your assets.

GLOSSARY

ABC Living Trust – a type of Living Trust for a married couple, which provides that when one spouse dies, the trust assets go into ongoing trusts for the benefit of the surviving spouse. The "ABC" refers to the three types of ongoing trusts that will continue for the surviving spouse's lifetime, generally limiting some of the surviving spouse's control and use of the assets.

All to Spouse Plan with Optional Disclaimer Trust – an alternative to an ABC Living Trust, which limits some of the surviving spouse's control, this type of Living Trust for a married couple gives the surviving spouse full control. If the survivor is concerned that tax will be due when she later dies, she could elect to fund some of the trust assets into a separate and more protected trust, called a **"Disclaimer Trust,"** which she can use but can't change. Where an ABC Trust requires certain ongoing trusts after one spouse dies, the All to Spouse Plan gives the surviving spouse the option of keeping all the assets in a fully flexible trust or funding some assets into a trust that could protect the assets from creditors and estate tax.

Authorization to Disclose and Release Protected Health Information – a document that allows a physician to release your health care information to those in charge of your assets and your health care decisions.

Beneficiaries – the individuals and charities you name in your estate plan to receive assets.

Beneficiary Designation – a document that determines who gets life insurance or retirement accounts after death.

Bypass Trust – an ongoing trust, sometimes informally called "Trust B," created by the terms of a Living Trust to hold assets after a spouse dies so the assets are protected from creditors and avoid estate tax. The surviving spouse generally can use the assets in the Bypass Trust, but has limited powers to direct who gets any remaining assets after the surviving spouse dies. A QTIPable Bypass Trust is a Bypass Trust with terms that enable a certain tax election to be made after a spouse dies so that for tax purposes, the trust has the attributes of a QTIP Trust, which are different than the attributes of a Bypass Trust.

Certification of Trust – a legal summary of the Living Trust, which can be relied on by anyone needing to know the essential terms of the Living Trust. The Certification of Trust will include the legal name of the Living Trust, the date signed, and the Trustee powers.

Certified Specialist – an attorney certified as a specialist in his or her area of practice by a State Bar Board of Legal Specialization.

Charitable Lead Trust – an irrevocable charitable trust structured to provide an income stream for a charity with the remainder going to children or other named individuals.

Charitable Remainder Trust – an irrevocable charitable trust structured to retain an income stream for the donor, leaving what's left at death to a charity.

Conservatorship – a court proceeding where the court oversees the management of assets, more often required if a person becomes incapacitated and does <u>not</u> have a Living Trust.

Deed – evidences ownership of real property, like a "pink slip" shows ownership of a car. Sometimes called a "Trust Transfer Deed," this type of deed transfers real property from the current owners to the Trustees of the Living Trust.

Durable Power of Attorney – a document that names someone, called an Attorney-in-Fact, to handle assets, such as retirement accounts, that are not titled in the Living Trust.

Dynasty Trust – a trust that lasts for more than one generation, continuing for the lifetime of children and then passing to grandchildren.

Engagement Agreement – a written agreement between the attorney and the client that explains the legal fee, costs and scope of the legal services to be provided by the attorney.

Estate Plan – a grouping of legal documents designed to control finances during life, and reduce expense and administrative hassle after death or incapacity.

Ethical Will – a document addressed to family, such as a letter, to express values, hopes and dreams for the next generation.

Executor – a person named in a Will to handle the administration of assets.

Exemption – the amount of assets that each U.S. citizen/resident can pass free of transfer tax during life or at death.

General Assignment – a document that transfers personal property, such as cars, jewelry and furniture, to a Living Trust.

Guardian of the Person – the person named in a Will to care for children under 18.

Guardian of the Estate – the person named in a Will to manage and control assets of children under 18.

Health Care Directive – a document that names an "agent" to make health care decisions upon incapacity.

Holographic Will – a handwritten, signed, dated and witnessed document that meets the requirements of a valid Will under state law.

Irrevocable Life Insurance Trust – an irrevocable trust that holds life insurance to remove life insurance proceeds from the insured's estate so that the proceeds are not subject to estate tax when the insured dies.

Irrevocable Trust – a trust that cannot be revoked or changed (without jumping through some hoops).

Living Trust – a written instruction manual that outlines who gets what at death and puts someone in charge upon death or incapacity. When assets are titled in a Living Trust, the person or institution named has authority over the assets, which helps minimize costly court involvement. The person who creates a Living Trust can change it as long as the person has legal capacity.

No-Contest Clause – a clause in an estate plan providing that if the person identified contests the plan, the distribution to that person is reduced or eliminated.

Parent-Child Exclusion – allows forms to be filed with the county assessor's office so that certain real property in California can be transferred between parents and children without reassessment. Generally keeps property taxes low upon a transfer during life or at death.

Portability – a provision in the current law that allows a married couple to use both spouses' Exemption after one of them dies if the surviving spouse makes an election on a tax return within 15 months of the first death. Portability has revolutionized estate planning for married couples and made couples re-think the use of Bypass Trusts. Before the portability of the Exemption, most couples created a Living Trust with a Bypass Trust to minimize estate tax when the survivor died.

Probate Court – a court that deals with the administration of estates, either during life when someone is incapacitated or at death.

QTIP Trust – an ongoing trust for a surviving spouse, sometimes informally called "Trust C," funded under the terms of a Living Trust after a spouse dies. The surviving spouse can use all income from the assets in the trust, but generally has limited use of the principal and limited powers to direct who gets any remaining assets after the surviving spouse dies.

QTIP-Protection Trust –a Bypass Trust after a tax election is made to convert it into a QTIP Trust.

QTIP Election – a tax election that can be made no later than 15 months after a spouse dies that will have certain tax ramifications at the death of the first spouse and at the death of the surviving spouse. The ongoing trust that holds assets for which a QTIP Election is made is called a QTIP Trust.

Qualified Disclaimer – a document indicating that an individual does not want to accept certain assets upon the death of another. Certain Living Trusts give a surviving spouse the ability to sign a "Qualified Disclaimer" so that certain assets can be funded into an irrevocable trust to minimize estate tax or to add creditor

protection. Section 2518 of the Internal Revenue Code of 1986 specifies strict requirements for Qualified Disclaimers.

Required Minimum Distributions – the amount that is required to be distributed annually from certain IRAs, usually based on the life expectancy of the participant or the named beneficiary.

Separate Share Trust – a type of irrevocable trust for children that keeps each child's trust assets separate, with expenses for each child coming from that child's separate trust account. Often used when children are adults and money is to be distributed in equal shares of fair market value.

Spousal Property Agreement – an agreement couples can sign to impact the character of their assets as community property or separate property.

Sprinkling Trust – a type of irrevocable trust that holds assets, typically for children, that allows the Trustee to distribute money to several people from one common trust account, without keeping track of who receives what. Often used when children are young and money is to be distributed to meet their needs without regard to whether each child is receiving an equal share of the trust.

Step-up Tax Basis – the adjustment of the tax basis of assets to the fair market value at date of death, which means that when the assets are sold at death, no capital gains tax will be due.

Survivor's Trust – an ongoing trust for a surviving spouse, sometimes informally called "Trust A," funded under the terms of a Living Trust after a spouse dies. The surviving spouse can use all the assets in the Survivor's Trust and direct who gets any remaining assets after the surviving spouse dies.

Taxpayer Relief Act – the American Taxpayer Relief Act of 2012, which "permanently" increases the Exemption to $5,000,000 (plus annual cost of living increases) and allows the surviving spouse to port the unused Exemption of the deceased spouse.

Transfer Tax – a tax imposed on the transfer of assets either during life or at death, called a "gift tax" if the transfer is during life or an "estate tax" if the transfer is at death.

Trustee – the person or bank in charge of the trust assets. Typically, the person who creates a Living Trust will be the initial Trustee and will appoint successor Trustees to act when the initial trustee becomes incapacitated, dies or is otherwise unable to act.

Will – a document that specifies who gets what at death and names someone to handle administration of assets and care for minor children. A **"pour over Will"** specifies that assets are to be put into the Living Trust at death.

Written Instructions for Distribution of Tangible Personal Property – a document that specifies who gets personal property like jewelry, furniture, art, clothing, and tools.

HOW TO TITLE ASSETS INTO A LIVING TRUST SO THEY DON'T GO THROUGH COURT PROBATE

Forming a Living Trust does not necessarily avoid probate. A Living Trust only avoids unnecessary court costs when the assets are transferred into the Living Trust. Transferring assets into the Living Trust ensures that the assets get distributed as directed by the Living Trust *without probate*. Those who form a Living Trust can easily transfer their assets to the Living Trust, often without hiring an attorney.

Bank and Investment Accounts (not IRA or 401k)

You can transfer bank accounts, including all investment accounts and small checking accounts, by completing the institution's form to change the owner to the Living Trust. Usually, the institution will give a new account number for the account held in the Living Trust. Be sure that the institution uses the full legal name, including the name of the Trustees, the name of the Living Trust and the formation date of the Living Trust (i.e., Susan Smith, as Trustee of the Susan Smith Living Trust, dated January 1, 2014).

Retirement Accounts (i.e., IRA, 401k)

Although all bank accounts can and should be transferred into the Living Trust, do not transfer an IRA or 401k to the trust without first seeking legal advice. Rather than transferring an IRA or 401k directly to the Living Trust, complete a document called a "Beneficiary Designation," which instructs the institution holding the retirement account how to distribute the account at the participant/owner's death. Be sure to include both a "primary beneficiary," to receive the account at death, and a "secondary beneficiary," to receive the account at death if the primary beneficiary is not living or otherwise does not accept the account. Never name "my estate" as the primary beneficiary or secondary beneficiary on the Beneficiary Designation of an IRA or 401k.

Tangible Personal Property (e.g., personal belongings, jewelry, furniture, tools)

You can transfer personal property, such as cars, jewelry, and furniture, to the Living Trust by signing a "**General Assignment**." The Trustee of the Living Trust will distribute the personal property as indicated in the Living Trust as long as the person creating the Living Trust signs a General Assignment to transfer the property to the Living Trust.

Stocks, Securities, and Bonds

For stocks held in investment accounts, see the instructions above under "Bank and Investment Accounts." For shares of stock held directly in a publicly traded company or for bonds held directly and not in an investment account, transfer the shares or bonds to the trust by contacting the "transfer agent" for each stock or bond issue and providing the agent with the full legal title of the Living Trust (the legal names of the Trustees, name of the Living Trust, and date it was created).

Owning all stock in a brokerage account simplifies life. Once the institution holding the account changes the name of the account to the Living Trust, all future stock purchases within that account will be controlled by the Living Trust.

IRC Section 1244 Small Business Corp. Stock and S Corporation Stock

Some stock, such as stock governed by Section 1244 of the Internal Revenue Code or certain stock of a so-called "Sub S Corporation," should not be transferred to a Living Trust without legal and tax advice.

Stock Options

Some companies offer their employees options to purchase stock. Owners of stock options should carefully read the company documents and contact a legal and tax advisor to understand what happens upon death under the terms of the stock options. Would the options simply lapse? Can/should the options be transferred to a Living Trust?

Real Property (e.g., homes, rental property)

You can transfer real property to the Living Trust by signing and recording a "**Deed**," sometimes called a "Trust Transfer Deed." The Deed transfers real property from the current owner to the Trustee of the Living Trust. A title company can often provide a form Deed. However, to avoid errors, an attorney should prepare the Deed. Once signed and notarized, record the Deed with the County Recorder's Office in the county in which the property is located. To avoid reassessment of the property and higher property taxes, sign a Preliminary Change of Ownership Report, printed from the county recorder's website in the county where the property is located.

"DUE ON SALE CLAUSE"

If you are obtaining a loan to buy a house or refinancing a loan, the lender requires a Promissory Note and a Deed of Trust, referred to below as **loan documents**. Many loan documents contain a clause, called a "Due on Sale Clause," which allows the lender to request immediate full payment on the note if the borrower transfers the property (i.e., sells the property or transfers the property into a Living Trust). Before recording a Deed transferring real property to a Living Trust, especially for non-owner occupied property such as rental property, it is important to obtain the lender's written consent. The consent should confirm that transferring the real property to the Living Trust does not trigger the "Due On Sale Clause."

Although some attorneys advise that lenders in California cannot enforce a "Due on Sale Clause" for a loan against an owner-occupied residence, cautious owners transferring their home into a Living Trust will first obtain the lender's consent.

ATTENTION CALIFORNIA HOMEOWNERS:

❖ All homeowners in California can apply to have a certain value of their home exempt from property tax. This Exemption is called a "Homeowner's Exemption." When transferring a home to a Living Trust, the county may require a new application for a Homeowner's Exemption. If the county does not send the notice to re-apply, contact the county assessor's office to confirm whether a new application for the Homeowner's Exemption needs to be filed.

Interest in General Partnership and Limited Partnership

You can transfer interests in a General Partnership and Limited Partnership into the Living Trust by signing an **"Assignment of Partnership Interest."** The Assignment transfers the interest from the currently named partner to the Trustee of the Living Trust. Carefully read the Partnership Agreement; the other partners

of the partnership may need to consent in writing to the Assignment of Partnership Interest.

Membership Interest in Limited Liability Company

You can transfer membership interests in a Limited Liability Company by first reviewing the "Operating Agreement," which governs all aspects of the operation of the company. Generally, the Operating Agreement will provide that membership interests are transferred to a Living Trust by signing an "**Assignment and Assumption of Membership Interest**" and an "**Amendment to the Operating Agreement**," which admits the Living Trust as a new member.

Sole Proprietorship

Many business owners choose to operate their businesses as a "sole proprietorship" rather than forming a partnership, corporation, or limited liability company. You can transfer a sole proprietorship to a Living Trust by signing an "**Assignment of Sole Proprietorship**."

Promissory Note

Whenever someone lends money, that loan needs to be documented by a signed Promissory Note, showing the date of the loan, the amount, the due date, and any other terms of the loan. You can transfer all Promissory Notes to a Living Trust by signing an "**Assignment of Promissory Note**."

Life Insurance

Life insurance owners often mistakenly name a spouse or child as the beneficiary of life insurance. Often, the most appropriate beneficiary of life insurance policies will be the Living Trust. If the Living Trust is not named as beneficiary, the Living Trust will not determine who gets the life insurance proceeds when someone dies. For example, if the life insurance names an 18-year-old child on the Beneficiary Designation form, the proceeds will be distributed to that child, who may decide to spend the money on a year in Europe instead of going to college. See Critical Fact #7 in Step #3 to review the benefits of forming a special Irrevocable Life Insurance Trust to hold the life insurance.

The life insurance agent can provide a blank Beneficiary Designation form to complete. By naming the Trustee of the Living Trust as the "primary beneficiary" on the Beneficiary Designation form, the Trustee of the trust will be able to distribute the life insurance proceeds to those named in the trust. When the sole purpose of the estate plan is to avoid the time and expense of probate, naming individual beneficiaries to receive insurance may suffice. However, to hold and protect the life insurance proceeds in trusts that the Living Trust creates, such as trusts for young children, consider naming the Living Trust as the beneficiary.

Interest in Professional Corporation for Dentists, Doctors, and Attorneys

Professionals such as dentists, doctors, and attorneys often conduct their practice in a business known as a "Professional Corporation." Shares in a professional corporation, or in a foreign professional corporation qualified to render professional services in California, may be transferred only to a licensed person, a shareholder of the same corporation, an individual licensed to practice the same profession in the jurisdiction or jurisdictions in which the individual practices, or to the professional corporation. Therefore, you may only transfer shares of a professional corporation to a Living Trust when the Trustee and all of the current beneficiaries are licensed in the particular profession.

Shares in a professional corporation can generally be transferred to a revocable trust only if the Living Trust instructs the Trustee to sell the shares and distribute the proceeds, and only if a licensed person will be in charge of the professional corporation. In addition, the Trustee appointed in the trust to handle the professional corporation must be licensed. For example, if the professional corporation is a physician's practice, the Trustee handling distribution according to the terms of the trust would need to be a physician. Additionally, the transfer cannot violate any written agreement, known as a Buy-Sell Agreement, between the partners of the professional corporation.

If all conditions of transfer have been met, you can transfer the professional corporation to the Living Trust by following these five steps:

1. Cancel the stock certificates for the previously issued shares.
2. Reissue new certificates for the same number of shares in the name of the trust.
3. Place the reissued certificates in a secure place like a safe deposit box.
4. Indicate the cancelled and reissued certificates in the corporate ledger kept in the corporate minute book.
5. Keep the cancelled certificates and copies of the reissued certificates in the corporate minute book.

OPTIONS FOR LIFETIME GIFTING

Gifting assets to others is more than just generous. For very wealthy families, lifetime gifts may save taxes. In fact, individuals can generally pass more wealth transfer tax free during their lifetime than they can at death.

The chart below demonstrates the many ways to gift and identifies the advantages and disadvantages of each kind of gift.

DIFFERENT WAYS TO GIFT	ADVANTAGES	DISADVANTAGES
Outright gift: write a check	Simple—won't need an attorney for smaller gifts of up to the Annual Exclusion ($14,000 limit per recipient in 2014) An easy way to get money out of an estate to save estate tax, especially if making Annual Exclusion gifts every year to many different recipients As long as the gift qualifies for the Annual Exclusion, no need to file any tax return	A child might not be mature enough to handle the money If you gift more than the Annual Exclusion to any recipient, you will need to file a gift tax return Gifts of more than the Annual Exclusion use up the Exemption that can be left transfer tax-free when you die; however, most wealthy people who anticipate their assets being subject to estate tax will benefit from using their Exemption during their lifetime rather than waiting until their death

DIFFERENT WAYS TO GIFT	ADVANTAGES	DISADVANTAGES
	Can make gifts up to the unused Exemption; however, if making gifts of more than the Annual Exclusion, typically it's best to use real estate or interests in a business rather than cash to best leverage the Exemption Can be used in addition to other types of gifts	
Outright gift; write a check in an *un-limited* amount to a qualified educational institution, like a college, or medical provider, like a doctor	Simple—won't need an attorney, but make sure the check is payable to the school or doctor, not to the child There's no limit to the amount that can be gifted free of transfer tax Can be used in addition to other types of gifts	For education gifts, the gift can only pay for tuition, not room and board If the child isn't going to college yet or doesn't have any medical needs, the child won't get an immediate benefit from the gift

DIFFERENT WAYS TO GIFT	ADVANTAGES	DISADVANTAGES
Gift to 529 College Plan offered by many financial institutions	Simple -—won't need an attorney Can gift five years of Annual Exclusion gifts in one year so that the assets can be invested immediately and grow outside the estate of the donor Tax benefits: no Federal income tax on gain in the account Professionally managed funds	Only for "qualified college expenses," such as tuition and board, not for supplies Investment options limited to those offered by the institution under the terms of its 529 plan Delays the benefits of gifting if the child is not ready for college
Gift into a "Custodial Account" for a minor	Simple—won't need an attorney. Most institutions will allow an account in which someone is put in charge of the use of the funds and the investments as a custodian under the Uniform Transfers to Minors Act ("UTMA")	Must terminate when the child is 18 (and until 25 in California) A custodial account can only have one beneficiary

DIFFERENT WAYS TO GIFT	ADVANTAGES	DISADVANTAGES
Create an educational trust (I.R.C. Section 2503(c))	Flexible—one trust can provide for multiple beneficiaries An unlimited amount of money can be funded into the trust as long as the trust funds are used for tuition, room and board, and supplies Simple to administer; needs minimal paperwork	Generally requires an attorney to draft the trust The trust has to terminate by age 21, unless the beneficiary has the right to terminate the trust within 60 days of 21st birthday. The trust can then provide that if the child does not withdraw then the assets stay in trust for the child (possible adverse tax consequence if the beneficiary has the power of withdrawal)
Create a so-called "Crummey Trust" and gift up to the Annual Exclusion	Same advantages as educational trust, except trust can continue beyond the age of 25 The gift can be used for any purpose as decided by the person you put in charge (called the Trustee)	Generally requires an attorney to draft the Trust Requires some annual administration including notifying the trust beneficiary that assets have been gifted to the trust giving them the right to withdraw the full amount of the gift (this is known as a "Crummey" notice, named after the legal case that allowed such gifts to qualify as Annual Exclusion gifts)

ENDNOTES

[1] A Release of Protected Health Care Information is required by the Health Insurance Portability and Accountability Act of 1996 ("HIPAA") and California Confidentiality of Medical Information Act (Civil Code Section 56 et seq.) ("CMIA") Public L. 104-191, 110 Stat. 1936.

[2] Under §2518 of the Internal Revenue Code of 1986, the term "qualified disclaimer" means an irrevocable and unqualified refusal by a person to accept an interest in property but only if—
(1) such refusal is in writing,
(2) such writing is received by the transferor of the interest, his legal representative, or the holder of the legal title to the property to which the interest relates not later than the date which is 9 months after the later of—
     (A) the day on which the transfer creating the interest in such person is made, or
     (B) the day on which such person attains age 21,
(3) such person has not accepted the interest or any of its benefits, and
(4) as a result of such refusal, the interest passes without any direction on the part of the person making the disclaimer and passes either—
     (A) to the spouse of the decedent, or
     (B) to a person other than the person making the disclaimer.........

[3] "Late funding" of the Bypass Trust refers to transferring assets into the Bypass Trust years after the death of the first spouse. Often a surviving spouse inadvertently fails to see the attorney in a timely fashion—an oversight that should be avoided. Even so, when compared to other types of Living Trusts, providing for a Bypass Trust can shelter assets from estate tax even if the assets are not put into the Bypass Trust until years after the death of the first spouse. Other types of Living Trusts require action within nine to fifteen months after the first death, or else all estate tax savings are lost.

[4] Wealthy families will generally want to pass wealth first in a trust to the spouse, then in a trust to their children, and then in a trust directly to their grandchildren when their children die. The family will hope that the trust for the children,

sometimes called a Dynasty Trust, will hold the assets for the children's lifetime and pass to the next generation free of a generation skipping transfer tax that would otherwise be due. Under the Taxpayer Relief Act, each person has an Exemption from the generation skipping transfer tax.

However, this Exemption from generation skipping transfer tax has special rules. When someone dies, and their Exemption is ported to the surviving spouse under the so-called "portability" rules of the Taxpayer Relief Act, the Exemption that is ported does <u>not</u> include the Exemption that would be needed for most trusts that pass to the children for life and then to the grandchildren—the Exemption from generation skipping transfer tax. Under the rules, if you want to pass assets to a spouse in trust, then to children in trust and then in trust to grandchildren and use your Exemption from the generation skipping transfer tax, you will generally need to leave the deceased spouse's assets in a Bypass Trust. Relying on portability, which ports the deceased spouse's Exemption from estate tax, but not from generation skipping transfer tax, to the surviving spouse, does not also port the generation skipping transfer tax Exemption. In sum, if your Living Trust provides for assets to go to your surviving spouse and then includes a Dynasty Trust for your children that will then flow to your grandchildren and your assets may exceed the Exemption, you should consider having a Living Trust that creates a traditional Bypass Trust for the surviving spouse.

ABOUT THE AUTHOR

Michelle's clients think of her as the "attorney with a heart." Her colleagues think of her as a mentor and leader in the estate planning legal community. A frequent guest on radio and TV, Michelle is certified by the California State Bar Board of Legal Specialization as a Legal Specialist in Estate Planning, Trust and Probate Law. She represents clients throughout California, creating custom estate plans for the unique needs of individuals and families. She also handles estates in Probate Court and assists in the administration of trusts after a death. Michelle obtained her Degree of Bachelor of Arts magna cum laude from the University of California at Los Angeles in 1980 and her Degree of Juris Doctor from the University of Southern California in 1983. She co-founded Lerman Law Partners LLP with her husband of 32 years, Jeffrey H. Lerman, Past President of the Marin County Bar Association. In addition to Probate, Trust Administration and Estate Planning, Lerman Law Partners LLP, known as the "Real Estate Investor's Lawyers[SM]," assists clients with real estate transactions, syndication, asset protection, loan workouts, litigation and business succession. Michelle and Jeff have four children and live in Northern California. Visit their website at www.myestateplancenter.com.

Made in the USA
Middletown, DE
01 November 2015